The Actor's Way

A Journey of Self-Discovery in Letters

BENJAMIN LLOYD

**ALLWORTH
PRESS**
NEW YORK

09   08   07   06   05   5   4   3   2   1

Published by Allworth Press
An imprint of Allworth Communications, Inc.
10 East 23rd Street, New York, NY 10010

Cover design by Derek Bacchus
Interior design by Sharp Des!gns, Lansing, MI
Page composition/typography by SR Desktop Services, Ridge, NY
Cover photo: www.paulgodwin.com

ISBN: 1-58115-447-X

Library of Congress Cataloging-in-Publication Data
Lloyd, Benjamin, 1962–
      The actor's way: a journey of self-discovery in letters / Benjamin Lloyd.
          p.   cm.
      Includes bibliographical references and index.
      ISBN 1-58115-447-X
      1. Actors—New York (State)—New York—Fiction.   2. Acting teachers—Fiction.
      3. Theater—Fiction.   4. Self-realization—Fiction.   5. New York (N.Y.)—
      Fiction.   I. Title.
      PS3612.L554A28   2006
      813'.6—dc22
                                                                    2006011283

Printed in Canada

TABLE OF CONTENTS

Summer: Study

Fall into Winter: Faith

Winter into Spring

RECOVERY

The following are a series of letters between my son Andrew Fallon and his former teacher, Alice Jones, with other letters and documents interspersed chronologically. I am grateful to the executor of Alice's estate, her sister Sarah Shelly, for permission to publish Alice's letters here. My gratitude goes as well to Andy, for being open to this project, and for all of his assistance in gathering letters and other documents.

One of the aspects of their correspondence that fascinates me is that it was, at Alice's insistence, almost entirely handwritten. Without the benefit (or curse) of the editing properties of computers, Andy's and Alice's edits are visible in the form of crossed out words and phrases. I have left these intact, sensing that there is something as revealing about what was almost written as there is in what was finally written. I also include occasional addenda in the margins of letters. The only editing I have done is correct some spelling errors. With Andy's help, I have footnoted some theatrical phrases or concepts that were clear to him and Alice, but might not be for a wider audience. I have done the same with some Quaker ideas, with Sarah Shelly's assistance. Later, as I include other authors, I have tried to be true to the difference between handwritten letters and other types of correspondence, like e-mail. Over the nearly year-long exchange of their letters and postcards, Alice's handwriting went from a graceful, classical script to a nearly illegible shadow of its former elegance. I occasionally guessed at words I wasn't able to decipher. These guesses are in brackets.

The book these letters and documents create is hard to pin down. But at the center of it is a gesture: the reaching out of a young artist to an older one, then a grasping of hands, resulting in discoveries about acting, teaching, and the Life of the Spirit. It was an extraordinary year for all of us. At the very least, it has brought me closer to my son. I hope you find it as interesting as I did.

—Linda Emlin Berkowitz
  Newton, Massachusetts

                                              July, 2006

12/26/04

Dear Teacher Alice,

~~Do you remember me? I was that screwup kid you cast as Peter in The Diary of Anne Frank in 1987 at Wallingford Friends School.~~

ITs ALL YOUR FAULT YOU MADE ME LOVE THIS. ~~NO I don't mean that I mean~~

Look, I don't even know you anymore. I last saw you in 9th grade. Who am I even writing to? This is for me because I'm feeling a little cracked. Acting ~~not its~~ is killing me. I can't remember why I loved it, why I keep doing it, but I have to keep doing it, I have to keep acting. There is nothing else for me. Its all I'm good at. And when I'm good at it, nothing else matters, all the pain goes away. But now, the pain isn't going away. I feel hollow, empty, vacant, detached. I think I have to stop acting. Forever.

~~Here. WTFS? I miss all the greasy the stage fields the~~ It made sense before. You made it make sense. Thats why I'm writing to you. It was ~~beginning~~

Look at this WHAT A FUCKING CLICHE I AM! TORTURED ACTOR BULL SHIT!!

[printed script in red felt-tip pen on yellow legal paper]

12/26/04

Dear Teacher Alice,

~~Do you remember me? I was that scrawny kid you cast as Peter in The Diary of Anne Frank in 1987 at Wallingford Friends' School~~

IT'S ALL YOUR FAULT. YOU MADE ME LOVE THIS. ~~No I don't mean that I mean~~

Look, I don't even know you anymore. I last saw you in ninth grade. Who am I even writing to? This is for me because I'm feeling a little cracked. Acting's ~~not it's~~ killing me. I can't remember why I loved it, why I keep doing it. But I have to keep doing it. I have to keep acting. There is nothing else for me. It's all I'm good at. And when I'm good at it, nothing else matters, all the pain goes away. But now, the pain isn't going away. I feel hollow inside, vacant, detached. I think I have to stop acting. Forever.

LOOK AT THIS WHAT A FUCKING CLICHÉ I AM!! TORTURED ACTOR BULLSHIT!!

~~How's WFS? I miss all the grass, the playing fields the~~ It made sense before. You made it make sense. That's why I'm writing to you. It was bigger than me and more beautiful than the world. You put us on a mission, we were your secret warriors of truth and beauty. Rehearsals with you were the best part of my day. They were ~~the island~~ the raft on which we were all escaping the same sinking ship. And we sailed to new worlds: Anne's Jewish ghetto, Gogo and Didi's haunted wasteland by the little tree, the forests around Athens with the lovers and Bottom, the strange inhabitants of the Welsh town Llareggub.[1] ~~I know it was just junior high~~ Those places and the people in them were in my dreams at night, and it seemed that everything else I studied at that school revolved around the play we were rehearsing. Even math. Scenes became a linear puzzle: the character pursues an objective by playing a string of actions on the other character.[2]

---

[1] These names refer to plays Andy was in at Wallingford Friends School (WFS) which Alice directed: *The Diary of Anne Frank*, *Waiting for Godot*, *A Midsummer Night's Dream* and *Under Milk Wood*.
[2] These are foundational concepts used by actors and directors to break down realistic scenes from plays into psychological units. These ideas get more attention later.

Now I'm rehearsing Florizel in *The Winter's Tale* for $225 a week before taxes, waiting tables at "Blue Angel"—the same stupid/trendy NYC restaurant I've worked at for six years—and drinking alone in my studio in Washington Heights. ~~It's the day after Christmas and I stayed in NYC to make some extra money~~ That's a lie. I stayed in NYC because I couldn't bear going home and facing those cheerful faces asking, "How's it going?" That's a lie too. ~~It's like my whole life is a~~ It's not the question that kills me— it's what I say in response: "Great!" The bullshit that comes out of my mouth when I'm around my family is intolerable (sorry to offend your Quaker sensibilities), as if I have to lie to them about how I'm doing because telling the truth is admitting defeat, and admitting defeat is an invitation for them to say, "So do something else with your life."

"QUITTING IS NOT AN OPTION!"

I will not do something else. I've been at this since I met you— that's 15 years. I got a B.F.A. in acting from Emerson in Boston, I'm freelancing with two agents, I do about two shows a year. Things are going really remarkably greatly.

Except that I broke down my closet door last night and I don't remember doing it. I visited some actor friends in the Village Christmas day, then came home and watched videos and toasted the season with some contraband Veuve Cliquot. By the second movie it was still light outside and I wasn't sleepy enough, so I resorted to the contraband Dewars. Then I woke up this morning with a swollen hand and a smashed-up closet door. ~~I think I might~~ Why am I even writing this to you? Who am I even talking to? This is ABSOLUTELY NUTS. You're never even going to get this if I even send it. You might be dead for all I know.

OK. This letter is a prayer to my memory of the last person I ever knew who made acting seem extraordinary, life-fulfilling. You started me on my way, and it has come to this. The thing that once saved me is now my oppressor. When I met you, it felt like I had escaped from a madman into a dollhouse filled with magic creatures, comfort, rich feeling, intelligence, and meaning. Now I live in that dollhouse, it's empty, and I think it might belong to the madman.

There's a still, small voice[3] inside me that says, "It is good to be an actor." You put that voice there. But I've forgotten why it's good to be an actor. Who cares? I'm a smart guy—shouldn't I help cure cancer, or fight injustice or something? Why bother, Alice?

Part of me hopes you get this letter and part of me doesn't. I don't even know what I'm asking you for. I know it's a long rant, forgive me. It's a difficult time of year, I'll be 28 January 18th ~~and my life sucks~~. I'm sending it to WFS because it's the last place I knew you. Do you still work there? If you write back, please tell me about your life. You were my inspiration once.

Sincerely,
Andrew Fallon

_____

[3]"Still, small voice" is a well-known Quaker phrase from a poem by John Greenleaf Whittier. Andy maintains he didn't recall its Quaker origin when he wrote it.

The Quad

January 5th, 2005

Dear Andrew,

I must tell you that I nearly threw your letter away after reading it. "It's all your fault" is not a good way to begin a letter that begs the reader's sympathy. I understand you're going through a rough patch now, but I must ask you for some decorum if we are to get to know each other again — and I'm not referring to my "Quaker sensibilities." I am as well-versed in familial "bullshit" as you are, a darn sight more so I should say, being in my seventies now. Write your concerns down plainly that I may think about them, and perhaps I may be of service to you.

The first order of business is your closet door. You broke it down for a reason, and the reason was that you were drunk. Before any other heartbreak or disappointment may be attended to, you must examine your closet door. What does your still, small voice tell you about that? What does it tell you about your relationship to alcohol? I gather from your use of the word

Swarthmore, Pennsylvania

[script in black fountain pen on embossed stationery, "The Quad, Swarthmore, Pennsylvania" printed on the top of each page]

January 5th, 2005

Dear Andrew,

    I must tell you that I nearly threw your letter away after reading it. "It's all your fault" is not a good way to begin a letter that begs the reader's sympathy. I understand you're going through a rough patch now, but I must ask you for some decorum if we are to get to know each other again—and I'm not referring to my "Quaker sensibilities." I am as well-versed in familial "bullshit" as you are, a darn sight more so I should say, being in my seventies now. Write your concerns down plainly that I may think about them, and perhaps I may be of some service to you.

    The first order of business is your closet door. You broke it down for a reason, and the reason was that you were drunk. Before any other heartbreak or disappointment may be attended to, you must examine your closet door. What does your still, small voice tell you about that? What does it tell you about your relationship to alcohol? I gather from your use of the word "contraband" that the spirits you were consuming were stolen. Is this true? What does your still, small voice tell you about stealing liquor from the restaurant where you work? (I hope you are not breaking into liquor stores.) Until you listen for an answer to these questions, there is no going forward for you. There will be no relief. The next time you may not wake up with a swollen hand. The next time you may not wake up at all.

    Do I seem alarmist? Good. My father was an alcoholic who died drunk in the snow on Girard Avenue on a cold, cold night in Philadelphia, 1945. I imagine you didn't know that about me. Like most alcoholic Dads he wasn't so unremittingly bad that I could simply write him off. He was terrible to my mother, but I loved him. You say I was the one who made you love the theater, Andy. Well, he was that one for me. He was a great bear of man who, I was convinced, was indestructible. He was not and neither are you. Has it occurred to you that there is a similarity between your relationship to acting and your relationship to alcohol? Both were once sources of great delight. Both lead you into worlds of fantasy. Both are now, as you say, your oppressors.

    But acting is <u>not</u> your oppressor. You are simply asking it to solve problems it can never solve. Indeed, asking it to solve those problems will only make those problems worse. Those problems are <u>your</u> problems Andy: yours to own, yours to solve (or at least be at peace with), yours to let go of. There are two roads before you: you can deal with your problems and be a happy actor, or not and be a miserable one. But I think you will always be an actor.

I remember you in 1987. A slouching, guarded seventh grader with piercing blue eyes shooting out beneath shocks of black hair. A sideways smile that eventually grew into a chesty laugh that lit up the room. What a joy it was to watch you drop your defenses. You became an exceptional young actor. How hungry you were to express yourself, to feel life, to grasp a passion and shake it to tatters. How instantly believable you were, and how wounded. How the theater began to heal you, and how sad that those wounds are still open, still festering, and that the theater is keeping them that way. The theater has done all it can for you, now you must turn your attention on yourself.

As I remember, you moved around a lot as a boy, didn't you? You were living with your mother at your grandparents' home in Newtown Square, Pennsylvania. Your parents were divorced. There was something going on with your mother—we, your teachers, were given information about it—but the nature of it escapes me now. You are an only child. You spent three years with us at Wallingford Friends' School before moving with your mother to Massachusetts. She was about to re-marry, I think. I am describing the rough shape of your childhood. This shape also describes the sinking ship your were escaping from with me. But you have remained on the raft, locked inside your magic dollhouse. The madman is your fear—fear of feeling what you must feel in order to escape the raft. No wonder you're lonely. Your fear is paralyzing you.

In my many years as an acting teacher and as a student of acting, and in my years of performing, I have made some observations about acting and the kinds of people drawn to it. Acting can be a refuge for lost children. They are lost because their families were transient and they had no reliable home, lost because of negligent parents, lost because of death, disease or addiction in the home. It was true of me, it's certainly true of you. But the greatest grief is not the wreckage at home, but the heartrending way the children react to it. A child will kill his own soul in order to try to gain his parents' love and save what remains of his home. In trying to salvage what they have no control over, these lost children become slaves to the dysfunction they live in, and so they develop no true "self." This is why you feel hollow.

Because the lost children are only permitted *permissible* feelings at home, feelings that will not trigger a horrific result of some kind, they crave free expression. Because there is always someone or something else more important

---

at home, they crave love. Because the wounds they have received have been inflicted with a sudden unpredictability, they crave order. Because they are not loved for who they really are (no one knows who they really are), they crave a cherished identity. And what is a role in a play? It is an opportunity to express yourself fully, within a story that has clearly described boundaries while a good teacher or director loves you for doing so. Best of all, you get to run away from your life and into this safe fantasy, which ends with a room full of people (usually including Mom and Dad) bursting into applause for you. This is why you feel that acting "saved" you. It saved you from your real life, which was quite painful.

So begins an intense, tender and necessary phase of narcissistic escapism that many adolescent and young adult actors pass through. The theater becomes an identity laboratory in which young people search for themselves beneath Helena's gown, Didi's old suit, Emily's white dress, Captain Cat's pea coat.[4] For some, a true self emerges, and I have watched astounded as a relaxed and confident young woman arrives at rehearsal one day, whereas before I had had a twitchy teenager on my hands. For others, the love of fantasy mutates into obsession, the pain required to birth the true self is too great, and an endless string of false selves begins, one dramatic role to the next. These become what I call "wounded actors." You and I are wounded actors Andy, but my wound healed long ago, and now I wear its scar like a talisman.

Your salvation is not on the raft. Your salvation is on the sinking ship, and you must row back and get on board, yes, even if it seems to pull you under while it sinks. If you do this and have some faith and ask for some help, I promise you, you will find the strength to swim ashore without any raft at all. You are the problem, not acting. You must end the narcissism by giving in to it. Make yourself the focus (not the characters you play). Once you heal, you may turn your attention to the world, which is where the actor's attention must always lie.

My goodness, listen to me. You can take the teacher out of the classroom, ~~but you cant take the~~ well, anyway. You may have found me at the right time, old shut-in that I am. I have been longing to speak.

Acting is good Andy because the world needs relief. But only healthy actors can heal a wounded world. Faith is the way you get there from where you are

---

[4]Here Alice refers to characters from the plays Andy mentioned in his letter, and she adds one: Emily is from *Our Town* by Thornton Wilder.

---

now. Here's a Quaker expression for you: seek until way opens. Way will open for you, but which way remains the mystery. I think you will get help from a very surprising source.

Have a happy birthday.

Yours,
Alice Jones

[printed script in red felt-tip pen on yellow legal paper]

1/11/05

Dear Teacher Alice,

Thank you for writing back. And thanks for the words of wisdom. But where are you? What's the Quad? Are you still at WFS? What about your life?

So I get the part about me being the problem, but I guess ~~what I'm saying is~~ what I want to know is, now what? I mean what do I do and how does it make me a better actor? The wounded actor thing is interesting, I've never thought about it. And yeah, I drank too much last month—obviously. So I'm easing up now. Point taken. Let me tell you about the rest of my life.

Tonight, I have to go back to rehearsal (*Winter's Tale*), which used to be a source of hope. Now it's a source of dread. With one or two exceptions, I hold most of the cast in pity—they remind me of me: aimless New York actors looking to suck every last bit of information out of each other in order to go up one more rung on the phantom ladder to . . . what? We all sit around and either regard each other from a wary distance, or celebrate some contrived connection with an explosion of fake enthusiasm. The truth is we are all desperate, and would stab the one next to us in the back if it would get us a network audition. New York, Los Angeles—it's like this everywhere.

And we never stop acting. We act at our restaurant jobs. We act during breaks. We act when we tell stories. We act when we go out for drinks. I even act alone in my apartment. Sometimes, after Letterman is over, I turn off the TV and pretend to be his guest. I can do this for about 20 minutes. Then I start to feel really crazy.

The only thing that unites us is our loathing of the director, a bitter old man who used to have a career in England until no one there could tolerate his evil temperament, so they kicked him across the pond to us. ~~He's a total~~ He directs through fear and humiliation. If rehearsal ends and no one's crying, it's been a good day. I took him aside during a break and asked him about a moment I'd been working on in the play. "Something's missing Bill, what is it?" I asked him. He replied "Skill" and walked away. After our first run-

HE'S SUCH A <u>BASTARD.</u>

through, when any good director will understand that the cast is essentially groping their way from one moment to the other, trying to remember lines, notes, blocking, etc., he began by telling us all that we had "shamed Shakespeare" ~~I mean what the fuck does~~ and then turned his ire on the actress playing Hermione and told her—in front of everyone—that she was inept with language and lacked any shred of physical grace. This is a woman with an established New York career, who is, in fact, <u>very</u> good. Her speech in the trial scene is a knock-out.

APPROVAL HE GAVE
BY SAYING THAT
SUCH AND SUCH A
MOMENT WASN'T
<u>AS BAD AS</u> THE
OTHER ONE

Here's when I realized I might have to chuck in the towel: Barbara, who plays Hermione, stood there and <u>took</u> it, then she nearly groveled for his approval for the rest of the note session before she retired to the ladies room to weep in a toilet stall. ~~I couldn't~~ We could all hear her in the rehearsal room. And no one <u>said anything</u>, we just milled around like guilty creatures. Finally, another actress went in to try and calm her down. When Barbara came out she smiled through her swollen eyes.

I am such a slave to this "career" that I sat and watched an episode of public brutality—I mean, it was like watching a flog-ging—and I did nothing. I am an accomplice to a crime.

That was three days ago. Before taking the subway home I went to Times Square. I just needed to walk around. I stood right in the middle of it all, on one of those islands made by the crossing avenues. I leaned against the statue of George M. Cohan and stared up at the insanity of light. I saw a nearly naked woman, reclining across a city block, leering at me with the question: "How BAD do you want it?" hovering above her. I saw a giant camera taking pictures of me. I saw news images of soldiers and guns, and words, words, words. It used to be a big deal when a billboard changed in Times Square. But now almost all of them change continually. You can stand there for an hour and not see the same collection of images twice. I thought of the "Matrix" movies. Maybe some ghastly artificial intelligence really is controlling our lives. When I began moving again, I noticed that George was covered in pigeon poop. I felt a deep affection for him.

My life is a series of small productions that begin with so much hope and promise, and end with crushing disappointment. The dis-appointment has nothing to do with whether or not the work was any good, ~~who knows what that~~ I've long since lost the ability to evaluate the theatrical worth of what I do. The disappointment is that Judy Casting Agent never came to see it, or that she did and asked Joe Chiseled Features to come see her, and not me. These productions are interspersed with endless plates of Thai Chicken Salad, dressing on the side please, and take the fish back, it's undercooked. I literally sleepwalk through my restaurant shifts, I don't know why they haven't fired me, I can barely hide my contempt for the customers I serve. And woe betide them if they ask me if I'm an actor. "Are you a casting agent?" I ask. When they answer no, I say "Then I'm just a waiter."

Today, I wish I was just a waiter.

The final blow came when, after that nightmare rehearsal, the guy playing Camillo asked me if I wanted to teach. He runs the education wing of the theater producing *Winter's Tale*. This is it, I thought, the end has come: those who can, do; those who can't, teach. I told him I'd think about it.

Riding home from Times Square that night I felt more alone than ever. It's amazing. I spend my days elbowing my way through this sea of humanity and I still feel like the last man on earth. Everyone on that subway wants something as badly as I want to be a successful actor. Everyone in this city is chasing a dream, and knowing that makes me feel very, very alone. Sitting across from me that night was a beautiful old woman with bright blue eyes and silver hair. She was reading a book of poetry. She glanced at me and held my stare. I had to look way. She reminded me so much of you. It felt like she had seen into my soul, the way you have. I think you're the only person who's ever known me.

Faith? I hope you're not going to throw a God thing at me (please don't tell me you've become a red-stater). I know all that was a big part of WFS but ~~I never~~ it's just not for me. But I thought Quakers didn't believe in Jesus, and that anything goes, or something.

Hey—can we do this by e-mail? My hand hurts. Glad to be back in touch.

Andy

☙

[script in black fountain pen on embossed stationery, "The Quad, Swarthmore, Pennsylvania" printed on the top of each page]

January 20th, 2005

Dear Andy,

No, I'm not a "red-stater," and I am offended that my mere mention of the word "faith" would have you leap to such a conclusion. In fact, the whole division of red and blue is absurd and depressing. I am an elderly Quaker, feminist, artist, and educator, and I have a deep and life-sustaining belief in God—a Judeo-Christian God at that—but that doesn't make me a narrow-minded ignoramus. And neither are the faithful of South Carolina, necessarily. My goodness, wasn't it us liberals who railed against bigoted stereotypes? And now look at us. If a person believes in God and isn't ashamed to talk about it, they are branded a "red-stater" or worse. What a sorry state, indeed.

Since you seem to have forgotten some basic tenets of the Quaker faith that guided three years of your formative education, allow me to give you a little primer. A Englishman named George Fox created what we call The Religious Society of Friends (Quakers) in the mid 1600s. The essential notion is that each human has some God inside them, so in violating another person, you violate God—unconditionally and in every instance. From this grows two radical beliefs: 1) that since God is inside us all the time, we can feel God all the time, He/She is our Inner Teacher, guiding us if we listen attentively and 2) since violating God is antithetical to our beliefs, we will not support violence of any kind.

Arrayed like great murals around the faith that there is "that of God in everyone"[5] are our Testimonies. These are ideas that have been borne out of our Quaker experience, and have been articulated by Quakers through the ages. The most well-known of our testimonies is the Peace Testimony, which leads us to our pacifism. Many Quakers have been jailed because of their refusal to take up arms or pay war taxes. Our Testimony of Integrity leads us to tell the truth all the time under any circumstances. This makes us a rather untactful lot, but quite willing to speak truth to power (and to tell a young man who drinks too much to deal with it). Quakers were years ahead of Western Civilization with our Testimony of Equality, which recognized the innate equality of the sexes in all matters. Many great Quaker leaders have been women. And Quakers were the

---

[5] A phrase from the Journals of George Fox.

---

16 THE ACTOR'S WAY

first abolitionists in the anti-slavery movement. Get Brinton's <u>Friends for 350 Years</u>, or Birkel's <u>Silence and Witness</u> and brush up on your Quakerism, my boy! If we are to continue our newly rekindled friendship, you will need to follow me as I show you how it all relates to being a good actor.

As far as Jesus is concerned, we each develop our own unique relationship to Him. Some of us draw strength from Him as an historical fact. For others, He is and has always been more Spirit than human, dwelling in us and beside us as our Holy Guide. And then there are some for whom He has neither gender nor any other human characteristic, but rather dwells in mysteries that defy words and symbols; He can only be felt. Quakers try not to argue about which words we use to describe Holy Experience, since words are human in origin, and therefore always subject to error. It is the Experience itself that matters.

But enough theology—let me write to you of my experience. I have a memory that may speak to your condition vis-à-vis your acting career. From 1974 until 1992, I had a small apartment in the West Village on Ludlow Street. I sublet it to university students from September to June while I taught at WFS in Pennsylvania. Most summers I sweltered in New York, taking classes and acting in one small thing or another. It was wonderful. I met many actors. One in particular made a lasting impression. I was about 45 or so, he was an elegant man in his sixties. We were in an evening of Chekhov one-acts. He had a permanently fixed smile on his face. It only changed when he was on stage. I gradually understood that he was a desperate man. He lived alone, and had been acting since 1962. After a show one night, I was about to leave the theater, but I heard a curious sound coming from the stage, a scratching sound. I peeked around the curtain and saw him. He had pulled the naked safety light next to a scenic desk and chair, where he sat writing postcard invitations to theatrical agents. "Bob, what are you doing?" I asked. He turned to me with that horrible fixed smile and said, "You never know. This show could be the one." He's dead now, but that image has haunted me for years.

The game you are playing with agents and casting directors in New York is an old one and it never ends. Its rules are formed by that ghastly intelligence on display in Times Square—its name is Commerce. Bob had become a <u>thing</u>, a thing that wanted to be bought, but he couldn't find a buyer, though he had been trying most of his adult life. No wonder the Puritans compared actors to prostitutes. It is a comparison we acquiesce to by playing this game. What a travesty that theater, which celebrates humanity above all other arts, should be so reduced to a mechanism by which people are bought and sold. If this is your life in the theater Andy, than you are right. Being a waiter is far more honorable and better for your soul. But here's where your letter made me angry.

Having that restaurant job is a blessing. It allows you to live and pursue your dream, clouded and confused though it is right now. But you denigrate it and show your gratitude by stealing bottles of champagne. You are in a play, an extraordinary play, in an extraordinary role. That is a blessing, diabolical director or no (I'll get to him later, the aberration). You wake up in the morning and do what you choose to do. Most people in the world get up in the morning and do what they have to do: to pay the rent, to feed the children, to survive. Others live out someone else's expectations. Never mind curing cancer Andy, you could be digging ditches. Who has put a gun to your head and said, "Be an actor?" You did, Andy, not me. So put the gun down and be an actor, not a thing to be bought or left behind. A thing will witness abuse and do nothing. A thing tricks itself up in slutty fashion and whines for attention. An actor acts.

You have a gift, I know, I saw it, and it may be buried beneath the muck and mire of your own circumstances right now, but it is there and it cries for attention. You can be an artist—not many have that blessing. Pay attention to your blessings lest you lose them all.

And how dare you disparage teaching. Did it not occur to you that I am a teacher? Did it not occur to you that I chose teaching over other leadings, leadings that called to me with the same ferocity that your journey calls to you? Did it not occur to you that the joy you experienced with me at WFS had something to do with my being a good teacher? Are you not blessed to have had good teachers in your life? How dare you trot out that vile phrase about "those who can't, teach." Those who can, do; those who excel, teach, my dear, confused little boy. That man has offered you yet another blessing, a way perhaps to live more fully in the art you love, and to give something back to others, and yet you sneer. Here is my one solid piece of advice for you. Accept his offer.

Acting is a service. So is teaching. What will you serve the world, besides appetizers and desserts? What will be your main course?

But now to your director. I assume you know that tyrants of his ilk are the exception not the rule. After encountering such a one as you have, it's important to remember all the wonderful directors you've worked with, how they make us better, how they fashion the world we get to play in, how they teach us in ways we only notice in retrospect. One of the great dangers of living the New York life you're leading is that you may come to view directors in general as The

Enemy, not to be trusted, only tolerated. I knew several actors like this. New York seems to breed a kind of cut-throat, me-firstness that inhibits good collaboration. If you have come to this, stop acting forever and pick up a creative form you can have more control of, like writing. But even then, you'll have editors to contend with. Acting and directing are the consummate collaborative art forms, and if we reject the possibility of working together in good will than we violate the discipline. You might as well draw pictures in a cave.

I have often felt that there is a missing class in the world of theater training. It is a class called "Collaboration," in which actors and directors study under the guidance of one acting teacher and one directing teacher—simultaneously. In this class, seldom taught to my knowledge, the focus would be on how we <u>work together</u>. The two teachers would watch scenes being rehearsed by student actors and directors, and speak to the challenges encountered. You would need two teachers, because actors and directors frequently have very different creative agendas, and a teacher from each discipline might ensure equal time for both points of view. They would need to be brave teachers who were willing to work out their own differences in front of the students. After all, it would be the messiness being investigated: I want this but you need that, I still don't understand after twenty explanations, why is it different from last night, etc. These are challenges that have no pat answers, but people with experience might be able to pass along strategies for more effective collaboration.

Right now, the task of working together is learned through trial and error in the rehearsal room, and the errors can sometimes leave lasting scars and mutual suspicion. Actors learn to act in classes without student directors, or worse, in which the young directors are forced to be actors. Most student directors learn how to direct in styles, and compose stage pictures and break down scenes, but not how to work with a brilliant but temperamental actor. Sometimes mistrust is bred in the classroom. I once took a class from an otherwise great teacher, a man who had studied with Sanford Meisner.[6] In this class, there were 12 or so actors, and four directors. One day, during a commentary on a scene, he said to the class with a wry smile "You see, what I'm trying to do

---

[6]Meisner, along with Lee Strasberg and Stella Adler, was an acknowledged master teacher of acting. With Strasberg and Adler, Meisner was part of the Group Theatre of the 1930s which had been deeply influenced by the teachings of Stanislavsky.

is make you director-proof. Because out in the real world, most directors don't have a clue." This was said in front of the directing students. I was mortified. What seeds were planted there?

And then there is the "dead dog" in the rehearsal room that nobody wants to talk about. The dog's name is The Familial Paradigm. As you know, I believe that many of us begin acting as a response to childhood trauma of some kind. I also believe we project surrogate roles on to each other in the rehearsal room. At WFS, I was "Mom" and you were my "children." All teachers play these surrogate parental roles to some extent, especially in primary and secondary education, but nowhere else is it as powerful as in the theater, where we are in the business of playing roles, of experimenting with identity.

This family paradigm is as true for directors as it is for actors, for most directors began as actors and then for various reasons decide they like it better on the other side of the table.[7] All of us bring our families of origin to rehearsal with us, and there we either try to escape from them, transform them, or kill them. Quite often, the more oppressive the family of origin, the more oppressive, or controlling, the director who comes from it. Because the director gets to play "Mom" or "Dad" now instead of the neglected child he once was, you have the potential for some child abuse masquerading as forceful directing. Actors can be just as lost in the Familial Paradigm, and act out within it in the most self-indulgent ways. Any diva you've ever seen is nothing more than a hurt little girl crying for more attention.

I'm not sure what the answer is to the effects of the Familial Paradigm. But I know that denying it only compresses its effects, and makes the paradigm prone to manifest in destructive ways. I feel that the more honest we are with ourselves about our own relation to the Familial Paradigm, the more we can have a sense of humor about it and us, and the less it will trap us. It will allow us to witness the eccentric and even irritating behavior common in the theater through a compassionate lens. On my best days, confronted with Bill your Bastard Director, I would have thought to myself, You poor, poor man. What happened to you all those years ago? On my best days.

Affectionately,
Alice.

---

[7] Alice means the rehearsal table behind which the director traditionally sits in rehearsal.

PS: It's Alice now. I'm not your teacher anymore.

PPS: Add to your reading list: *The Drama of The Gifted Child* by Alice Miller, and *Healing the Shame That Binds You*, by John Bradshaw.

DEAR ALICE, 1/28/05
    YOUR LETTER ROCKED
MY WORLD! I'M READING
THOSE BOOKS. THINKING
ABOUT DRINKING (OR
NOT). SAID YES TO TEACH-
ING - SORRY ABT DISSING IT.
I NEED HELP w/THAT TOO!
WILL WRITE SOON, LONGER,
and w/DECORUM.
        YOUR STUDENT 4 ever
                    ANDY
PS - What's "The Quod"? DO YOU HAVE PHONE?
            E-MAIL?

Alice JONES
    THE Quad
    338 PLUSH MILRD
    WALLINGFORD, PA
                19086

[printed script in black ballpoint pen on postcard, image of Times Square on reverse]

Dear Alice,

Your letter rocked my world. I'm reading those books. Thinking about drinking (or not). Said yes to teaching—sorry abt dissing it. I need help w/that too! Will write soon, longer and with decorum. Your student 4 ever. Andy.

PS—what's "The Quad"? Do you have phone? E-mail?

[printed script in black ballpoint on plain white ink-jet paper]

Dear Alice,

Thank you for your extraordinary letters. ~~If I had known what I was hoping for, it would have been more than that, if you know what I mean. Things here have been~~ They have knocked the wind out of me, which is good for a windbag like me.

Snow is falling. I used to love a great snow storm, when everything stops and we are forced to live in the throes of Mother Nature. I remember how you surprised us one day when a storm arrived in the afternoon. We came expecting to rehearse those strange gothic one-acts by Don Nigro—I can't remember their names now. But they had to do with ghosts and generations. You told us to bundle up, and off we went into the snowy forest behind the playing fields, the flakes coming down fast. "Find a tree you like and stand next to it!" you shouted, and we did, spread out from each other amidst the grey and white, knee deep in snow. Then you shouted "Begin!"

My heart is beating fast here and I feel like crying. The memory of the fog of my breath shooting out in blasts as I called out my lines, the image of all of us sneaking from tree to tree as we built the scene, and you standing still in the snow—it's all somehow very painful to me now.

I wish I was writing you the "Everything's better" letter—but I'm not. Everything's more fucked up than ever.

I was fired from *Winter's Tale* last night. It was notes after a preview and Bill went after Barbara again, and before I knew what was happening I stood up and said "Lay off her!" ~~I had been drinking~~ I wasn't drunk. The rest is kind of hazy, but it involved a shouting match between me and him. I was being restrained, I broke free, I slapped his face, he fell down, I left, they cancelled the show, I was fired. Daniel, the education guy, begged the theater (Total Artist Group or TAG) to let me teach—so I have that job. Bill never came back. Rumor is they fired him too, but I don't know and I don't care. I'm so embarrassed—slapping a guy in his sixties. I've never been fired from anything before. I don't know what's going on with me.

I'm doing a test. It's been 19 days since I've had a drink. If I can get to a month then it's not a problem. I fucking hate it.

I hate the teaching too. I have a beginning acting class once a week on Wednesday nights. I feel like such a fraud. I have these eight people, half of

THE ACTOR'S WAY

whom are older than me, and once a week they show up and stare at me with these expectant faces, like I have something to tell them. I'm using "Acting One" by Robert Cohen. Do you know it? I made them all buy it, and each week we do exercises from the next chapter. I mean, I have to work through the exercises with them—I'm not <u>teaching</u> them anything. It feels like we're all learning to fix carburetors using the GM manual. We'll do an exercise and then they all turn to me with those expectant faces, as if I'm supposed to explain something to them. I usually say something inane like "Well, that was interesting wasn't it?" Expectant faces. "Okay then!" I say, "Let's move on to the next one!"

I feel like I could be doing this better, I mean I'm really convinced I could, but I don't know how. I keep thinking about what you said about teachers, and I keep thinking about my teachers, but all I feel is weepy and nostalgic. I'm a box full of experience, but I've lost the key. It's agony.

I found a quote that made me think of you. Last year Bob Keeshan died. He's the actor who played Captain Kangaroo on TV. He was speaking to some gathering in Vermont and he said:

"Through the years, I have dwelled upon the concept of extending circles of influence, as with a pebble in a still pond, emanating from a skilled teacher and reaching to worlds the teacher is unaware of. But in the beginning is the teacher, and eternity is influenced by his ideas as those ideas are passed on and on and on, beyond light, beyond years, beyond light-years. What a noble and awesome power you have, a power beyond the reach of virtually every other calling." That's the kind of teacher you are, the kind of teacher I aspire to be. I'm so far away now.

For the record, the notice you received about my Mom was that she was being treated for depression. Beginning in 1987 she started taking some pill and saw a shrink twice a week. It got worse, then it got better. She would curl up in her bed and stay there, sometimes for a day or two. My Grandma would try to intercept me before I got to her bedroom. "Not a good time right now, darling" she would say. But sometimes I got to Mom before Grandma got to me. Mom would try to escape from me by pulling the covers over herself. My Grandparents would pull me off of her, kicking and screaming. Yeah, I guess you could call it "quite painful."

To fill in the blanks, because I don't know how much of this you know: we came to Pennsylvania from San Francisco, which is where my Mom and Dad were divorced. Dad's still there, re-married to Sharon The Trophy Wife, with two new kids: Danny's 12 and James is 9. After the separation, Mom and I lived in

Oakland where I went to a school and was picked on by these tough kids. Dad's job moved us around a lot: before San Fran was Las Vegas, before Las Vegas was Chicago where I was born. So I guess I fit your little "lost child" profile pretty neatly. But you knew that already, didn't you?

I don't know what to make of those books you "assigned" me. They strike me as bogus self-help nonsense. The whole thing about toxic shame in the Bradshaw, about playing roles in your family of origin. It makes me sick to read it. I thought I was so unique. But I'm just another kind of cliché—the child of dysfunction. It's so embarrassing. The Miller book seems a bit more scholarly, at least. Her book was viscerally painful to read, that point that both she and Bradshaw make that the suffering person's salvation lies in the abyss, in confronting and experiencing the pain (returning to the sinking ship, you say). She says depression signals the proximity of buried feelings. Bradshaw describes buried feelings as wild dogs in the basement.

The wild dogs escaped and I broke down my door. They escaped again and I slapped a mean old man. Now I have them back down in the basement and I feel depressed to the point of imitating my Mother. Thanks a lot. So I get it. Now what do I do? WHAT DO I DO ALICE?

I've lost acting, ~~I've lost~~ I'm not sure about the booze. I'm pretending to be a teacher, and I'm waiting tables almost every day. Is this my life? I'll kill myself.

Confront the pain??? What am I supposed to do, just call up my Mother and say "Thanks for fucking up my whole life! Sorry Dad left you and you were so sick, but what about me, you selfish bitch??" Call up Dad and say "What was I to you—baggage?? You dragged me from place to place before splitting for some younger babe. Guess I was too much of a burden." Is that really gonna solve anything? Is that what ~~you you're~~ your favorite authors are suggesting? ~~Why did you~~ *Here's* the pain—it's spilling out on to these pages and filling up this miserable little room I live in. Thanks, Teacher Alice—thanks for the help.

[script in black fountain pen on embossed stationery, "The Quad, Swarthmore, Pennsylvania" printed on the top of each page]

February 15th, 2005

Dear Andy,

If you think you're angry at me now, you may need to use a punching bag after you read what I'm about to write (but do be careful of your sore hand—is it still sore?). You are right where you need to be, you are feeling what you need to feel. The ice around your heart is melting, and that tender organ is free to react to the bracing effects of sunlight and air. It throbs now, only because it's not used to being in the world. Those dogs are true feelings and they are swimming, pulling your raft back to the ship where the healing will happen.

Your attack on Bill was, in part, the angry son's revenge on the negligent father. That's not to say that Bill's behavior didn't deserve a reaction of some kind. It surely did, but not yours. You behaved badly and you deserved to be fired. I hope you've learned your lesson. But yours was an extreme case. The Familial Paradigm's negative effects are most often much more subtle, masked as they are beneath the already odd behaviors in play at rehearsal.

Before you rip up this letter, here's the good news: you <u>have not</u> lost acting, you've just put it down for the moment. Soon you will board the sinking ship and begin the hard work of salvage. On it, you will find the key for that box of experience, that box you can teach from, which will reveal you to be the extraordinary teacher you are. And I will not forsake you in the face of your anger, you are not angry at me. I am the surrogate for Linda, your mother.

You have entered the necessary darkness. Much depends on the choices you make over the next several weeks. But remember, you are familiar with darkness. You took a skill learned in the darkness of the shadow of your mother's depression—acting—and transformed it into a source of joy and creativity. That was a remarkable thing you did, it made you a wonderful actor and a brave, brave boy. Your darkness is an attractive part of you, Andy. It's why I cast you as Puck, who is not the happy cherub so many mistake him for. Remain brave and do not forsake the art which saved you. Though it cannot save you now, it needs you to return when you are whole and healthy. The fact that your impulse to act is rooted in pain does not invalidate that impulse. If you accept that painful source, your art will be forever grounded in something real and pro-found, and soon that source will not ache so much. It will simply be. You will understand your art as having saved your life, and your celebration of it will be evident in every role you play, in every class you teach. Your Light, which once flickered, will burn brightly, borne and nurtured as it was in darkness. You will be a beacon for others.

In the midst of the seeming chaos in your life now, you need a place to be still. Get yourself to a Meeting. Rest and listen to the rustling of the Spirit, feel the nudges of the Inner Teacher, hear the ministry of others.[8] And ask for help. You need someone, or some others, with you now. It can't be me, I'm too far away and anyway I'm not skilled in the right techniques. You know what I'm talking about. Get the help you need, and you will get through this and flourish.

Now, about your acting class—get <u>rid</u> of that book. I know Bob Cohen, I took a couple of workshops with him. He's a good man with a deep concern for acting and how it's taught, but I believe that in writing these books (and he's made a small fortune out of them) he's misrepresented an essential aspect of how acting is learned. There's that other one too, "The Practical Handbook" or whatever, written by Mamet's students. There's nothing practical about acting, or the teaching of it. It's not learned in a straight line and it cannot be taught out of a book. Bob will tell you he never intended the books to be used the way you're using them. Hogwash. They are laid out and presented as textbooks, and published by a textbook publishing company. They are textbooks, and they lead to deadly teaching. Especially in academic environments like universities (or WFS, for that matter), where students are trained to study books and the intellectual oppresses all other forms of learning, these acting textbooks trick students into thinking that they contain answers. They rob the teacher and student of flexibility and they throw focus on themselves (i.e., the textbooks), and off of the relationship between teacher and student, which is where the alchemy of teaching acting is revealed.

Yes, alchemy. There is something magical, spiritual, transcendent that happens in a good acting class. The "Practical Handbook" equates acting with building a chair, and states flatly that there's nothing mysterious about acting. What? If I wanted to build a chair, I'd build a chair. I prefer to drag my students out in the snow for reasons I don't quite understand and have them rehearse in the woods. The mystery of that experience led to a wonderful production (by

---

[8]Alice refers here to experiences common in Quaker meeting for worship, in which worshippers sit quietly seeking the Divine. When an experience is moving enough, a worshipper will stand and speak to those gathered. This is called "vocal ministry."

---

the way, the play was called <u>Glamorgan</u>), and the power of it has stuck with you for years, even though it was born from a hunch when Teacher had little else planned and was fed up with her usual curriculum.

Acting textbooks (and the whole movement to "demystify" acting and turn it's study into a series of building-block steps) are yet another way commerce is killing our art. There are so many young people out there like you, who want answers to their pain, and hope for their dreams. Someone's got to make money off you, most likely the person who tells you acting's as easy as 1, 2, 3, and all you have to do is take their class, or buy their book. But acting goes 32, 572, 6, 2.85, actually. So help your students understand what they're <u>doing</u>, but not at the expense of what's illogical, paradoxical, magical about acting. Isn't the magic why we started acting in the first place?

Look, here's how you use a book like Cohen's, or any book that purports to be a text for acting teachers. You comb through it for exercises you like, or concepts you like, or turns of phrase, and you steal them for use in your class. You add them to the exercises, sequences, and scenes you've stolen from me and every other teacher you've ever worked with, and from it all you create your curriculum. And yes, it is <u>yours</u>, you do not need to footnote exercises (though if it comes up, it's sometimes interesting to describe an exercise's journey from teacher to teacher). The curriculum is yours because no one has ever combined it in the same way, and because <u>you</u> are teaching it.

There are two essential questions to answer before you teach a class: 1) what does this class mean to the institution offering it? If your institution is like most, when you ask them, they'll say something vague like "You know—it's a beginning acting class," as if that means something reliable to anyone. But some may have some specific parameters, and some may wish you to teach from an already established curriculum (those jobs are the hardest, like making love according to someone else's directions. If they hand you a textbook, walk away). Anyway, I assume you've had that conversation with TAG.

The second and more important question is, what does teaching this class mean to you? What does "beginning acting" mean to you, Andy Fallon? What should a novice be able to do after eight, ten, fourteen weeks with you? What do you want them to feel about acting? Understand about acting? This is another reason why using a textbook is such a bad idea. Those expectant faces are searching <u>yours</u>, they want <u>you</u> to teach them, not Bob Cohen's book. Don't bother wondering whether you're any good, it's a waste of time. The man playing Camillo asked you, you agreed, and there you are. Teach, and don't look back. In a good acting class there is a dynamic collision of souls. Open your soul to your students and they will open theirs to you. If you watch them closely, and listen to them carefully, you will know what to say.

You see, it's not so much what you teach, but <u>who you are</u>. Searching, compassionate and open souls make the best teachers. Such is your soul, Andy. Mr. Keeshan's extraordinary pebble doesn't drop from any book, it drops from the teacher's very Self. Those expanding circles of influence are driven by <u>people</u> and their spiritual energy. Your students want <u>you</u> to move them, the way I moved you, and you never will if you give your authority to a book. Here is a link to Quakerism. Almost 400 years ago, George Fox and his friends were so fed up with preachers beating everyone up with the Bible, they would burst into church services and debate the priests, yelling "I know what the book says, but what canst thou say, friend?" The Quakers have always regarded the Bible as a record of a <u>moment</u> in history, not the end of revelation. For us, the revelation continues in every moment of every day. And so it should be for the actor and the acting teacher. The Quakers rebelled against ministers who used Biblical interpretation to oppress their followers, and so should you rebel against any codified dogma in the teaching of acting, especially if it comes out of a book. The reliance on textual analysis has crept into the theater, where some will pour over scripts like Talmudic scholars, trying to divine the playwright's intent, and delivering judgments based on their "discoveries." Enough! Get up on your feet and walk it around, I say. Quakers believe the essential aspect of our religious experience is the <u>experience itself</u>. And so it is true of the actor and teacher: your experience is what you must draw on, then you will be speaking from your heart, and the hearts of your students will resonate.

The key you're missing is called permission. Will you give yourself permission to teach the acting class you <u>want</u> to teach? Will you risk bringing your <u>self</u> to the fore, risk the messiness and uncertainty of human contact?

A fear any teacher has is the fear that they will come to an impasse and not know what to do. And yet this is precisely the moment great teaching is made of. For in this moment the teacher has nothing to draw on but her wit and Faith—Faith that whatever she chooses to do, it will amount to something. Countless times in countless classes I have met that moment, and each time my heart raced a little faster. Each time the students knew (cunning creatures) that something was up. ~~Each time~~ Most often, we surprised each other with an authentic encounter. Once I stopped having to be so <u>planned</u>, and began trusting the moment more, trusting the dynamic collision more, real encounters and real learning took place in my classes. Suddenly, I was right there, with them, I knew it and they knew it. And off we went. Which is not the same as being disorganized, no, you should know where you want to take them. But leave room for the unexpected visitor, the sudden detour.

An acting class should be an adventure, the students should feel like they're never sure what's going to happen one moment to the next, even if you do. Then you and they are fully alive, all senses tingling, hearts beating faster, eyes open wider, impulses arriving quickly. This is the actor's state: preparing for spontaneity, one of a million paradoxes that inform acting and the teaching of it.

Or you can just say, "Well, let's end a class a bit early today. See you next time."

These letters exhaust me! Hang in there, boyo. The world is turning and the sun will rise tomorrow. Face the east!

Love,
Alice

PS: And for God's sake, don't use monologues for a beginner's class. Monologues are an advanced actor's challenge. Beginning actors need to *share* the experience (which is what acting is—a shared experience). Monologues only scare beginners back in to bad habits, generalities and indication. Go directly to scenes, or if your class is long enough, use short scenes, change partners, longer scenes.

PPS: Reading list addenda: "An Actor Prepares" and "Building a Character" by Constantine Stanislavsky. These are the only required reading for any acting teacher in the West.

[script in black fountain pen on embossed stationery, "The Quad, Swarthmore, Pennsylvania" printed on the top of each page]

February 25th, 2005

Dear Andy,

I'm so worried about you. Please write soon. I have become attached to our correspondence, can you tell? I wish you would write more frequently though. The following is humorous. Perhaps it will cheer you up.

Had a bit of a row last night. We must be cut from the same cloth. Or maybe you and your outbursts are having a deleterious effect on me. In any case, I caused a scene at one of the awful lectures they sponsor here. I live in one of those assisted-living situations where America sends its old people to die, especially if they have no immediate family, and I do not (at least no one I'd care to move in with, even if she'd have me.) It's called The Quad, or as I refer to it, The Pod.

This man was lecturing us on the wonders of the Internet, and he kept using the phrase "There are two kinds of people . . ." to set up some silly point he was making. Andy, he must have used that phrase ten times in a half an hour! And I don't think he was trying to be funny! Finally I raised my hand and said "There are indeed two kinds of people, young man, those will listen to this nonsense and those who won't!" And I hobbled away to my garret feeling very silly. I am a confirmed Luddite. What was I doing at a lecture about the Internet anyway?

It's not a garret. It's an apartment off a hallway that looks like any Ramada Inn. It has my number on it: 855. It's comfortable, with meals provided and a little button by my bedside in case I need nursey to take my temperature. Phones are a bother and God help me no "e-mail." I have few friends, which is my own damn fault, since I can't bear the chit-chat and small talk that passes for true communication here. I own a little car and I can get out to see a play or a movie every now and then. But I hate going alone, and inviting someone from The Pod isn't an option, since it means I'd have to put up with them.

I was forcibly retired from WFS in '98, and part of my golden handshake was this place. It's all paid for and I am well taken care of. First-rate medical care, if necessary, and all that. It's founded on "Quaker values" (whatever that means). I molder away with fellow aging Quakers and others. My Meeting is close by, and I am involved there in a variety of ways. I should be grateful. But I could still be working, and I'm bitter that they made me leave.

I so miss teaching. I embraced being the magical "Mom" for all of you. It was a role I cherished. Indeed, it was all I had, and I have been in deep mourning for it since it was taken from me almost seven years ago. You can tell how badly I miss it by the ridiculous length of my letters. You embraced me as my little foundling, and we bonded in a fiction, a fiction which sustained us both. And it's dawning on me as I write this, that it is my job, too, as well as yours, to create sustaining bonds in <u>life</u>, bonds that continue after the graduation, the retirement, the closing night.

There is a wiry old woman who lives down the hall from me named Edith. She's from salty New England stock, and I like her, except that she's got a memory problem. She keeps asking me to play bridge and I've told her every week for nearly two years that I don't know how. I even sent her a letter, which said "Dear Edith, please tape the enclosed on the inside of your door! Love, Alice." The enclosed said "Alice Jones doesn't know how to play bridge." What a dunce I am! She knows I don't know how to play bridge! It's just her way of reaching out, and I've been too crusty to see it.

Resolved: Edith Murphy and I will go out on the town next week.

Did you see that Andy? That was your ripple sending me into action. Thank you, my foundling boy.

Love,
Alice

DEAR ALICE —
HAPPY ST. DAVID'S DAY!
DOWN IN YOUR OLD
STOMPING GROUNDS!
TEACHING BETJER,
STAN'S THE MAN! 2 AUDITIONS
last WEEK! 2 MANY EX-
CLAMATION POINTS ON
THIS POSTCARD!! MORE LATER!!)
I LOVE YOU!!! ANDY
PS YOUR leHers are AWESOME!!!

3/1/05

ALICE JONES
THE QUAD
338 PLUSH MILL RD.
WALLINGFORD, PA
19086

[block letters in blue ballpoint pen on postcard, image of Village Cigars on West 4th Street, NYC, on reverse]

3/1/05

Dear Alice—Happy St. David's Day! Down in your old stomping grounds! Teaching better, Stan's the Man! 2 auditions last week! 2 many exclamation points on this postcard! More later!! I LOVE you!! Andy

PS Your letters are AWESOME!!!

Dear Andy,
Your postcards are comical—
here's mine. E and I are taking
in Renoir sp. exhibit. As you
say, awesome! Letter next
time, please. How are classes?
Lve, AJ
P.S. Good boy for remembering St.
David. Eat some leeks.

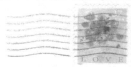

POST CARD

Andrew Fallon
28 W. 83rd St.,
#4B
New York, NY 10024

[script in black ballpoint pen on postcard, image of Philadelphia Museum of Art on reverse]

Mar. 10

Dear Andy,
Your postcards are comical—here's mine. E and I taking in Renoir sp. exhibit. As you say, awesome! Letter next time, please. How are classes?

Lve. AJ

PS: Good boy for remembering St. David. Eat some leeks.

[printed script in blue quick-dry ink on yellow legal pad]

3/20/05

Dear Alice,

Glad to see you're getting out. I'm especially glad you're getting out with a friend. Your last letter frightened me. I had this
image of you locked away in this sad place, making yourself more
alone than you need to be. Your gift comes to life when you share
it. It's what makes you such a great teacher (maybe it's that Quaker
thing too . . . ?). I think things will look up for you at The Quad now
that you have a buddy.

I've become very interested in this Family Paradigm business.
It's grown on me. But there's a part of me that hates it, hates the
idea that something painful is at work in my creative life and I
don't even know it. Maybe, as you say, if I embrace it instead of
running from it, I'll feel differently about it.

I love what you wrote about actors and directors, but you left
something out: power. What makes a director like Bill so terrifying
is that he's in control. Unless you work for some hippy-dippy
artistic collective, the director has the power. When's the last time
you heard anyone in the theater complain about a tyrannical actor?
Our misbehavior is infantile because the power relationship in the
rehearsal room is set up to have us follow, to take direction. You're
right, most often this is freeing, and a good director sends us off to
play and invent without the threat of reprimand. It's when the
power, the domination, becomes more important to the director
than the collaborating that you move from the Dad and The Kids, to
the Warden and The Prisoners.

I remember at Emerson thinking this guy (who was on the faculty) directing us was obsessed with passing judgments. "No, no,
no it's all wrong" he would say with this little smile on his face.
Wrong? It's not wrong, asshole, you just didn't like it, which
doesn't make it wrong. It's one of the reasons I reacted so nega-
tively to Daniel's invitation to teach. So many teachers I've known
are invested in hierarchy and passing judgments. Maybe this is just
a university thing, but I never want to be like that. I want to go on
a journey with my students, leading them on an exploration in

which they discover the best parts of themselves. I want to be a Dad that isn't afraid to get down on the floor and play with the kids.

And who gives the director notes??? Actors are continually evaluated, judged and adjusted by the long line of directors they work with if they're lucky to have long careers. Yes, more often than not those evaluations have positive outcomes, and directors help us improve. You write of experience, my experience has taught me that no one can harm an actor more than an abusive director. Poor directing can cripple actors by sabotaging their confidence, by instilling paranoia, by making fear the generator for their choices, not joy. How do directors improve? Who evaluates them? It seems to me that the person with the most power in any construct should be evaluated most closely, but in the theater the opposite is true. Within the traditional production process, directors are evaluated least. Alright, I'm done, I'll take the chip off my shoulder now.

Mom came to visit and we had it out. ~~We went for a walk in the park and one thing led~~ It's too exhausting to get into here. Years of buried shit came to the fore, just pouring out of me. She said "I always knew this day would come, when you'd confront me like this. It's okay." And that just pissed me off more. Anyway, I'm seeing a shrink. God I hate admitting that. I feel like such a stereotype: fucked up young actor has to see a shrink. Dad's paying. Because of my Mom's depression I have a thing about shrinks. I HATE IT. And the doctor I see, Dr. Kayne, is like the black hole of human interaction. She just sits and stares at me. Just what I need, more expectant faces.

DO YOU THINK I'M FULL OF HATE??

And I'm going to meetings. I went 21 days without a drink, decided it wasn't a problem, got whacked on St. Patrick's day, rode the subway home in between the cars, was met at 125th street by two transit cops who, instead of arresting me, drove me home. One of them even told me where a nearby meeting was. I want to find him and thank him. God I long for a boring month. ~~The meetings are~~

So my class is totally different now. I did what you suggested with the Cohen book. I don't own that other one. I finished with my group from the winter session on March 18th. We did some scene work and it was okay. I feel bad for them—like I ripped them off unintentionally. I begin with a new group next Monday.

Winter into Spring

39

What does beginning acting mean to me? First of all, it should
be fun. Otherwise, why bother? When people are enjoying themselves they open up, they risk more, they fear less. I say a pox on
grim acting classes. So we will begin with a couple of weeks of
Andy's favorite wacky theater games and exercises. Just so you
know, I intend to use Zing-Boing and Repetition,[9] which I learned
from you. Expect no acknowledgement, nor remuneration—I am, on
your advice, thieving from you. I will also employ some work I
learned at Emerson called "The Viewpoints"[10] plus some exercises
based on The Grid—a pattern I learned at a movement workshop I
took at The Judson Church downtown. I want them to understand
right away, before we get to text, that acting is a total experience,
both body and mind. If they can begin to make creative choices
physically, they are more than halfway there. Around week four I'll
assign scenes. Weeks five through ten will be scene work. No textbooks. And yet . . .

HOW MANY
MORE BOOKS
ARE YOU GOING
TO ASSIGN
TEACHER ALICE?!?

Should I make them read <u>An Actor Prepares</u>? I resisted reading
that book, after you "assigned" it. I thought—Oh God, Stanislavsky.
But damn if it didn't seem fresh, vital. And what an easy read! That
amazing theater they have class in, with a small army of techies to
make scenery for Tortsov's exercises. Those students who remind
me of my own, who remind me of me (I'm the argumentative one—
Grisha). Kostya's experience of going blank during a scene, his
moment of connection, his mistakes in preparation—been there,
done that. And what Tortsov says about acting seems so current.
But I'm confused, who is Stanislavsky in the book? And how does
an acting teacher use it? I'm tempted to do the "Madman at the
Door Exercise"—is this wise? And what about units and objectives?
I have my own vocabulary for those ideas—but should I assign the
book and use his?

---

[9]These exercises are described in the appendix.

[10]A rehearsal technique for the theater originated by Barbara Dilley in the 1970s, developed by Mary
Overlie at ETW/New York University and made famous by Anne Bogart/SITI Company. It does not
rely on the traditional psychological focus of realistic acting training but rather trains in multiple
dimensions of physical awareness such as space, time, rhythm, shape, etc.

"Building a Character" was tougher. Started great, with that amazing description of Kostya creating his first character, and the effect it has on him, the students and Tortsov. Then the middle part put me to sleep. Endless descriptions of gymnastics exercises and tempo-rhythm. But the book comes to life at the end, when Tortsov goes off about theater etiquette. Beginning with the chapter called "Stage Charm" it feels like he decides to let loose about some stuff that's been bothering him for a long time. It's inspirational.

While I was buying those books, I bought some others. You mentioned Mamet in one of your letters, so I bought a book he wrote called <u>True and False</u>. Scary. But ~~true~~ worth reading. One moment I shouted "Yes!" as I read it, the next I shouted "Asshole!" and threw it across the room. The best thing about it is his belief, which I share, that the only reason to take an acting class is to learn to be an actor. I think he would take a dim view of your whole Family Paradigm theory. He makes it sound like he thinks acting can't be taught, and that anyone who says they're an acting teacher (especially if they work at a school) is an automatic fraud. He calls Stanislavsky nonsense and his system a cult, but his descriptions of acting training are actually descriptions of <u>bad</u> acting training, which he generalizes as <u>all</u> acting training. And yet, he calls actors the bravest people he knows (I agree) and says that acting is a service for an audience (I agree). He tells us to speak up, even though we're afraid (I agree). He's maddening.

I also bought <u>The Way of the Actor</u> by Brian Bates. It's a trippy book in which he investigates the actor's "lineage," while at the same time interviewing famous actors like Liv Ullmann and Charlton Heston. The interviews bothered me for reasons I can't put my finger on, but his ideas about the actor's lineage are cool: we are descended from shamans and priests. Our original function was spiritual, but when organized religion came to the fore, it pushed theater into the gutter. It made me think about your observation that the Puritans thought of us as next to whores. He describes how actors have been marginalized in every culture since the middle ages. So my inner sense of otherness, of not belonging, of being an outsider, is reinforced by our culture's relationship to the occupation I've chosen. He implies that if we were able to reclaim our position in the culture as spiritual agents (sacred actors, he calls us), we would tap into great creative energy and heal some old wounds. I like how that sounds.

He also says that we are all actors—that we all know how to act. This gets back to Mamet's position that acting cannot be <u>taught</u>. It's a suspicion I've had for some time: we all innately know how to do this. The teacher somehow helps us remember. In my brief experience as a teacher, I feel more like a facilitator. It's as if I try to show my students a doorway and say, now walk through it. I can't tell you what's on the other side, but I can promise you will learn something about acting, and yourself, if you do it. I know it's scary, feel the fear and do it anyway. And when I imagine myself being that kind of facilitator to my students, guiding them through a revelatory experience, I feel very warm inside. It moves me. I want to get to class now!

But instead I have to serve up some lobster ravioli in saffron sauce and crème brulee for dessert. This job is a blessing this job is a blessing this job is a blessing—my new mantra, even if I don't believe it.

One other key thing I'm going to do with my class—I'm going to employ a buffer. I always found the beginning of class awkward, unfocused—both as a student and as a teacher. I'm going to invent some ritual to begin class with each time, some way to acknowledge the transition from "out there" to "in here." Not sure what it will be, but we need a way to begin, to focus, to come together. Perhaps a moment to be still together. Oh yes, and no monologues!

Four pages! I'm catching up to you Alice!

Love,
Andy

PS: More postcards please! How about South Street and Vet Stadium? I dare you!

[script in black fountain pen on embossed stationery, "The Quad, Swarthmore, Pennsylvania" printed on the top of each page]

April 1st, 2005—Happy Birthday to me, I'm seventy-two!

Dear Andy,

If your first letter made me angry, then your latest made me weep for joy. I am astonished, amazed, overjoyed that you are attending Meetings! God works through others in our lives, and surely the Light shone brightly through the blue uniform of that wonderful policeman who showed mercy on you that dark night. (On a side note, I find the shenanigans that attend St. Patrick's day utterly repulsive, always have). And how did he know where the nearest Meeting was? It never occurred to me that there might be Meetings for Worship in your neighborhood. Do you think he was he a Quaker? How unusual <u>that</u> would be, not sure how he would handle the Peace Testimony though.

There should still be a wonderful Meeting adjacent to Stuyvesant Square Park on east 15th street, the New York Friends Center, or something like that. See if you can find it, and as you wait in the expectant quiet imagine me sitting there on a hot First Day" in July in 1974. We weren't very different. And if the Inner Teacher nudges you with a message to share, notice how you feel in the moments before you rise to speak. It is the same feeling you have before you walk on stage, or before you give the St. Crispin's Day speech¹² (never mind Olivier and Branaugh—I still remember your rendition thirteen years ago). If the ministry is true and it speaks to those in worship with you, you may feel as you did when you played Harry: your heart may race, your throat may open, your back may tingle. This is the proof of George Fox's divine experiment. Your experience of the Divine is the only proof you need. Your experience as an actor and a teacher is the only authority you need. Those feelings are the Divine at work within you and through you.

The only difference between a Quaker in vocal ministry and an actor in the throes of his passion is the venue and the recognition of divinity at work. Some Weighty Friends¹³ will disagree, but I believe when a human speaks from that passionate place, in which the motive for speaking is <u>felt</u> as well as thought,

---

¹¹For centuries, Quakers refused to use the names for the calendar months or days of the week, believing them to honor cultures deemed ungodly. Thus Sunday became First Day. This usage has generally died out.

¹²From Shakespeare's *Henry V*.

¹³This phrase refers to the generally older and more experienced members of a Quaker community.

when he speaks from the place that makes him <u>quake</u> (where we get our nick-name: our trembling as the Divine flows through us), then he is in touch with the Divine. Good actors connect what they say to something urgent they feel. This is the root of the Quaker Testimony on Integrity: we say what we mean. This is something you have always understood intuitively.

I am quite interested in the two books you mentioned. I will buy them tomorrow when E and I take tea downtown. But especially your friend Bates, who sounds like my kindred spirit. It is a sad truth that religions generally have been hostile to artists, sadder still that none more so than ours: The Religious Society of Friends. The early Quakers were deeply committed to removing themselves from all that was "worldly," in order to live lives solely focused on the continuing revelation of God. Anything that was a distraction was tossed out. This not only meant performances of all kinds, but also bright colors and any household item that might be deemed "decorative." As extraordinarily brave as we were in the seventeenth and eighteenth century, I'm afraid we were a dour lot, too.

This anti-aesthetic bias continues in the modern era, and is not the special province of Quakers, either. Try getting a university to acknowledge the value of teaching creative process. Regarding your Emerson professor: yes, universities are deeply invested in passing judgments, in handing out grades, in assessing "outcomes." But fortunately a human being in an acting class is not a muffin, and it's not as simple as combining the right ingredients, baking for six weeks and voila: an educated actor emerges. There is no "assessment protocol" that can accurately quantify what happens to a young person in an acting class. Acting—the subjective nature of evaluating it, the centrality of the inter-personal dynamic to its success and the mysterious ways it manifests in students—is anathema to universities, which more and more depend upon a kind of education that can be reduced to a few pungent paragraphs in a tenure dossier. This kind of "score card" learning favors the natural and social sciences, which don't mind being reduced to easily quantifiable outcomes. I took my turn teaching at an Institute of Higher Learning, perhaps I'll tell you about it some-time. It's not only the Puritans who look down their noses at us. And if you're an actor as well as a teacher, you're doubly dubious. We play for a living. Most people suffer for a living and detest their jobs. We actually enjoy, even cele-brate our jobs. For this, we have earned great suspicion and occasional con-tempt, which is merely the uglier mask of envy.

I confronted the Quaker anti-aesthetic bias early on. My mother, a devout and somewhat repressed Friend, struggled with me for years over my bur-geoning love for acting. My father had saved enough money to buy a small vacation home in Mt. Gretna, Pennsylvania, a resort community about an hour's drive west from Philadelphia. He called it "The Retreat." It was a three-room cabin nestled amidst a confusion of other small cabins clustered around a lake. Before he drank all the money away, we were able to spend summers there, with him driving out on the weekends to join us.

And there was a theater there, one of those shed theaters in which the audience sits under a roof, but the sides are all open—a kind of indoor/outdoor experience. Every Saturday night, he would take Sarah and me to see whatever show the summer stock company was performing that weekend, while my mother stayed at The Retreat and fretted about the pernicious effects of the stage. This is when I miss my father most, when I let myself remember those nights, sitting in his lap eating salty peanuts and drinking watery lemonade, and laughing and laughing, laughing as he laughed, the kind of laugh that gets everyone laughing, laughing as the lemonade spilled on my dress and his pants from the concussive movements of his great belly, laughing as those magical people on that stage transported us: him, my sister, and me. That was it. From then on, I was determined.

But my mother was equally determined. Even as I began to act in small roles at the Gretna Playhouse in the summers of the late forties, she never came to see me in anything, never asked me about my experiences there. After my father's death, my acting became a deep spiritual connection to him. I honored him in the milieu where I loved him best. It helped me repress memories of the drinking, the yelling, the running away. Still, my mother refused to support me, and hustled us home to Germantown for First Day Meetings, where (she thought) I could reflect on my wayward passion. But in those seething teenage years, all I saw reflected in Worship was art and my own yearning. Sitting there in the quiet, dressed in my simple thread,[14] I saw inside me a great bird of many colors who took light in and increased it a thousand fold, then sent it blazing into the hearts of others.

Eventually, I fell in love with a young actor from New York who proposed to take me back to the Big City with him after Mt. Gretna's summer season of 1950. After the requisite nervous breakdown, I had an opening.[15] I knew that the journey of my life was going to be the struggle to bring that bird forth, without

---

[14]Quakers traditionally used "plain dress"—clothing that was functional and lacking any ostentation. "Simple thread" is another phrase for it. Alice's mother adhered to this custom, which has also generally died out.

[15]An opening is a Quaker term for a sudden Divine revelation. A great opening led George Fox to begin forming what became the Religious Society of Friends.

---

denying who I was. I knew running away to the Big City with my flame of the moment was a denial of who I was. I was, and I am, a member of a Monthly Meeting[16] I love, and I had a family, though it was small and broken. I had to keep that bird alive, while I attended to my family and my spiritual life.

I don't know why, but every spiritual journey I've ever read about or heard of involves sacrifice. Not "sacrifice," as in I'll try not to swear so much, but a brutal Wrestling with the Angels sacrifice, sacrifice that leaves you lying awake at night in tears because all you have is grief for what you've given up, sacrifice which costs you something very precious, very dear. To this day, Andy, I'm convinced I could have been Anne Bancroft, Shirley MacLaine, Judy Dench—any of the great actresses of that generation. There are movies I still can't watch, because I'll think, There she is, the one who got my career. And I could have done it better.

But cue the orchestra please, here's the Happy Ending: once you decide to stop wrestling the Angel, once you say I give up, the Angel kisses you, holds you in her arms and heals you, imparting a strength and joyous certainty that you have done the right thing. You will always want what you gave up, but in the Angel's embrace you will see that what you have is so much greater. The Angel will put you on your feet in your life as it is, and say, "Go now, and do your work, and be happy." There is strength in surrendering.

Maybe I could have been a movie star. Maybe that would have made me happy. Who knows? What I know is that I went to Swarthmore, got a wonderful education, and ended up teaching at Wallingford Friends'. It was a career which fed and nourished me beyond my wildest dreams. It's where I met all of you. Later, I realized that the time was right to take that glorious bird for a walk, and I started studying and performing again. I loved it just as much. Not bad. That bird had lost none of her shine. Really—what did I ever give up? I'll never know.

Damn this arthritis. Edith's here and says there's an interesting lecture. We'll see. More later.

Love,
Alice

☙

---

[16]A Monthly Meeting is a regular gathering of Quakers, who conduct a Meeting for Business once a month and generally gather to worship once a week.

[e-mail to Andy 4/3/05]

hey you. um I just wanted to say thanks again for oscar nite with benefits. cant decide which I liked more—the food, the you or the deep talks. as far as that goes ive been thinking about it and I think your right. its cool to thank god when you get an oscar. ill try to remember that when my time comes. and lets not make any definitions now okay? lets just follow our hearts together. words mess things up sometimes esp. early on. Um um um um um um soooooooooo but I cant stop thinking about you. Xoxoxoxoxoxoxo xoxoxoxooxoxo maya

ps—where's my poem?

[email to Maya Pelli 4/3/05]

here's your poem. see you tomorrow?

All It Takes
You showed me that little scar on your forehead
and I flashed the bruise
where my last love had been
wounds beside the aching place
still propelled us forward
wobbling like toddlers
so fearful and so brave

I can't decide what's better or worse:
The tumult in my head when we touch
or the exquisite longing when we're apart
when you think should I call
when I wonder if you're thinking
of calling
and I wonder if I have any right
to wonder

It's very adult
this in-between place we're in
I smile when I think of us
and our honest confessionals
I think of all it takes
to trust another human being
and let go
taking comfort in the sleepy love
of cats
and God

[blue felt-tip pen on torn yellow legal pad]

Hey Alice—   4/6/05

   Um, I meant AA meetings. But thanks for the deep spiritual message, and for the story about The Retreat. It made me think about how little we know of our teachers' lives. They present themselves to us as if hatched from a huge egg, fully adult and spouting wisdom (or bullshit, depending). How much more rich it is to know of the forces that made you who you are, the forces that turned you into the woman I met in 1987. When you can connect what a teacher says or does in class to that person's life somehow, it makes what they say or do have a power beyond words. Then you are listening to the result of someone's life.
   When it rains, it pours—teaching is getting really interesting, auditions suddenly out of <u>nowhere</u> ~~and I think I~~ there's this girl. Gotta run! More later (I promise!)

Andy

[script in black fountain pen on embossed stationery, "The Quad, Swarthmore, Pennsylvania" printed on the top of each page]

April 10th, 2005

Dear Andy,

I'm embarrassed about my "meeting misunderstanding" and have nothing else to say about it. Though I do hope we may continue to explore the relationship between acting and spirituality, and that you will visit the Friends' Center. I will say, however, that the buffer you seek to employ at the beginning of your classes is really a tiny Meeting for Worship and a grand idea.

Snatches of letters will not do at all. You have no idea how I look forward to our correspondence. It has been a mixed blessing though, for through it I can see my own loneliness more clearly. I have been getting out a bit more though, however . . .

I must find out who engages the speakers here and have them fired. Tonight's silliness came in the person of a perky young woman who wanted to talk about "Sex After Sixty." Appalling! At least have someone who's had sex after sixty share their insights with us. This woman, Dr. Somebody or other, had the gall to hand us charts and diagrams, as if we didn't know how the items in question were supposed to work. Edith turned to me and remarked dryly, It's really just a question of declining pace and friction, isn't it? Then we had a terrible case of the giggles and had to leave. We went to her place and drank beer and watched baseball. Beer is supposed to make you sleepy, but tonight it's done the opposite to me—so on we go. You've given me the chance to spill some beans I've been saving away.

You asked about making your students read Stanislavsky. How badly we want textbooks for acting, even when we know it's no use! Of course you shouldn't assign Stanislavsky to your students. This is part of that first question: what does this class mean to the institution offering it? Your students, I assume, are New York amateurs and semi-pros just starting out, or trying something new. There are more immediate things to attend to than reading Stanislavsky, especially if you only have ten weeks. You can mention him and his books, and those who are interested may read him, if they wish. Now, if you were teaching in some serious graduate program, then I might feel differently. But even then, you would not be assigning this book as you might a textbook. If you did, you would send poor Constantine spinning in his grave. You might assign it within the context of a longer training process as required reading, because his ideas form the source of all Western realistic acting training for the last hundred years. Even better, you might assign it in such a way that those reading it would be on the lookout for their own associations with the story he tells.

Stanislavsky was deeply suspicious of fixed ideas, especially ones which purported to make rules for art. When he finally got around to writing down his own ideas (something he did as a last resort to make money for his beloved Moscow Art Theatre), he took great pains to write something that could never be used as a textbook to teach from. He disliked the notion that anyone would refer to the "Stanislavsky system." He viewed his ideas as having grown organically from nature, the result of years of observation, both of his own struggle as an actor and the struggles of his peers and students. He constantly admonished his students to make their own "systems," knowing that he was exploring a moment in a continuing investigation (rather like the Quaker belief in continuing revelation). And so he wrote a novel about an acting class. He's hard to find in it, because he is two people: he is Kostya (the diminutive nickname for Constantine), and he is Tortsov. He is in the book as he was in his life, both student and teacher.

Remember that Stanislavsky was an actor for many years, and for many years a rather mediocre one by all accounts, including his. So his ideas are born out of direct experience, and the humility of having tried, and failed, to become better. Usually theory comes before practice. Stanislavsky flipped it around: he created theories from observing—and experiencing—the practice of acting. I imagine him as a kind of Fred Gwynne or John Lithgow—a tall, slightly awkward actor with a kind of child-like curiosity. His clumsiness was legendary. They pushed in all the chairs when he entered a room, or he was sure to trip over one.

The kind of acting he was writing about was brand new. We call it realism, but it was uncharted territory then, the popular Russian theater of the late nineteenth century having been a kind of histrionic melodrama. Stanislavsky's books are the story of an aesthetic revolution in the theater. Ibsen and Chekhov had a bit to do with it, too.

The story of how his books came to be published is almost as interesting as the books themselves, and sheds light on the trouble you had with the second one, Building A Character. Stanislavsky set out to write one book, which he called An Actor's Work On Himself. This great book formed the expression of an approach to acting that was holistic, synthesizing the mind, the body, and the spirit. But in the desperate times of the early Soviet Union, he sent the first half of the manuscript to his American publisher for quick money, rather than wait until he got around to finishing the whole thing. This first half has come to us as An Actor Prepares, and left us with the mistaken impression that it is the complete "system." Because its main focus is the psychological workings of the actor, Stanislavsky has been mis-apprehended as promoting training which favors the psychological over the physical. This isn't true.

The second half of his book, what we call Building a Character, introduces the physical. But we seldom read it, because in reading An Actor Prepares, we think we know Stanislavsky, so why bother; and because Building a Character is a more difficult read. It's difficult because it was pieced together from notes and drafts years after Stanislavsky's death. I've always felt that this is part of why it doesn't hang together quite as well as the first book. Read Sharon Carnicke's book Stanislavsky in Focus for more about the transmission of his ideas, and the extraordinary influence of his translator Elizabeth Reynolds Hapgood.

And let me draw your attention to the chapter called "Communion" in An Actor Prepares. Here, Stanislavsky speaks directly about the spiritual energy generated and received by actors. He calls it Rays, or he uses the Yogic term prana. Throughout both books, Stanislavsky uses the word "spirit" and its derivatives over and over. There is no question but that he felt there was a mysterious component in the actor's power that went beyond "mind" and "body." Don't leave spiritual exploration out of your curriculum, but how you present it is up to you. Let me suggest all those exercises we did on communicating without words as a way to begin. Once you awaken the student to the possibility that we give and receive spiritual energy, that is enough. It is up to each person to arrive at their own conclusions—or to keep the investigation open.

If you go to Meeting for Worship, reflect on Stanislavsky's Rays there. Notice the ways in which the gathered Meeting[17] vibrates with spiritual interconnectedness. Remember your best moments on stage, or in class, and ask if those vibrations are not of the same Source. Stanislavsky never mentions a religious affiliation, and it doesn't show up in his biographies, either. One would assume he attended Russian Orthodox services before the revolution. But his open contempt for aesthetic dogma, his reluctance to have others use his writings as holy writ, his belief in the ongoing evolution of the theater (in which he saw himself

---

[17]A gathered meeting is one in which the Holy Spirit is collectively felt by the entire congregation. Gathered meetings are considered rare and special.

---

as but a part of a continuum), his deep focus on the actor's experience and his mysterious spiritual nature lead me to believe he was a Quaker in spirit. You write of lineages. It is my hope that you feel yourself in his lineage, so often misunderstood, and that you commit yourself to his high ideals for the art you both love.

Gracious, it's two in the morning. Good night. By the way, they blew up Veteran's Stadium last year. Good riddance.

Love,
Alice

April 20
Dear Andy—
E and I are taking
in a game. What
weather! Phils are
clobbering Mets. A
fine day indeed. Cat
got your tongue? Write
back. Love, AJ 100191180

Andrew Fallon
28 W. 83rd St.
#4B
New York, NY 10024

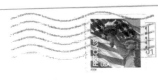

[script in black ballpoint pen on postcard, image of Citizen's Bank Baseball Stadium on reverse]

April 20

Dear Andy—E and I taking in a game. What weather! Warm and sunny. Phils are clobbering Mets. A fine day indeed. Cat got your tongue? Write back! Love, AJ

May 10
Dear Andy—
Surprised? E and
I made a pilgrimage
with Sam. I think
he's counting me.
Intolerable. As is
your silence. Have I
upset you?
    Love, A.J

Andrew Fallon
28 W. 83rd St., 4B
New York, NY 10024

[script in black ballpoint pen on postcard, image of Geno's Steaks,
South Philadelphia on reverse]

May 10

Dear Andy—Surprised? E and I made a pilgrimage with Sam. I think he's
courting me. Intolerable. As is your silence. Have I upset you?

Love, AJ

[typed in Times Roman, single spaced, on stationery with "TAG, Total Artist Group, Chelsea, New York City" printed on the top of each page]

5/15/05

Dear Alice,

Sorry, sorry, sorry. I've been totally in the weeds since receiving your last letter. As you can see, I've graduated to a keyboard. I'm sitting in TAG's Education Office. I've carved out a couple of hours and I have my triple grande, hazelnut cappuccino steaming in front of me. I can't promise to match your output, but here goes . . .

Don't worry about mixing up the meetings. In fact, the meetings I go to share something in common with Meetings for Worship. I remember really enjoying the weekly Meetings we went to at WFS, and sensing . . . something, when I wasn't passing notes to someone and trying not to laugh. My meetings have a spiritual foundation—which I'm just beginning to explore—and a kind of spoken ministry, but it's much more focused on the issue at hand: addiction. There's a lot more talking at my meetings. But what happens there is amazing. It's happening to me. And there's a strange connection between George Fox, Stanislavsky, and Bill Wilson.[18] Bill became deeply spiritual, resisted dogma, focused on experience, wanted others to take what he made and "pass it on."

But the meetings themselves . . . amazing. I think I'm not supposed to talk about it, the anonymity thing. But your story about your Mom and Dad and Mt. Gretna reminded me of the stories you hear in The Rooms (that's short for The Rooms of AA). Intense little slices of life that manage somehow to transform you. Stanislavsky's Rays bouncing off the walls and burrowing deep inside. Anyway, it's some kind of new beginning for me, I thought I'd hate it but I really love it. It's my new secret mission.

I'm sleeping a lot, and I have these bursts of feeling. Yesterday I wanted to hug everyone on the subway. I stood there with this insane smile on face. I'm sure everyone thought I was stoned. Then last night a commercial made me cry.

---

[18]With Dr. Bob Smith, the founder of Alcoholics Anonymous.

A freaking commercial! It was about cell phones! It was all about connecting to your family and I just lost it. It was like I was demonstrating over-the-top crying to a class. I held on to my pillow and sobbed. Then *Scrubs* came back on and I laughed like a hyena. I feel like Zack Braff's character in *Garden State*—numb for years and then alive. What the hell's going on? Dr. Kayne says I'm releasing buried feelings. Whatever.

Your story (history? her-story?) made me think of some questions—or queries as you Quakers call them. Why did you never marry? And the other one is, if you hate The Quad so much, why don't you just leave? I'm sure there's some small apartment you could find. Wouldn't that be better than living in a place you hate? And if you do stay, is there a way you could find to relate to The Quad positively? You say you're bitter because you're not working. Well, why not work at The Quad? Do your gifts only apply to young people? Do you not have anything to offer the community you live in now? Just some food for thought.

And yes, you did upset me. Why did you lie to me about having a phone? You have phone, Alice. I called The Quad and asked. The lady said, would you like me to put you through? I said no. I was too taken aback. That's part of the reason it's taken me a while to write you. I had to get over whatever that was about. Why are you cutting yourself off, from me, from the world? Maybe there's a simple explanation. If there is, I'd like to know it.

My second "semester" has come to a close. The difference between it and the first one is night and day. But I still have so far to go. Some observations:

My "buffering ritual" consists of a chime I ring which signals the beginning of class. Then we form a standing circle in which we move from scattered to focused. At the beginning of the circle, we all finish gossiping, or telling jokes, we stretch on our own and we gradually come to "neutral": feet under hips, arms hanging at sides, energy flowing up through the top of the head. We move our focus from the floor in the center of the circle to each other—we check in. After about three classes, I noticed that we all had our mouths closed. So I asked everyone to just drop their mouths open into a kind of "duh" face. I asked them to breath through their mouths and see each other. Boom! People smiled, laughed, squirmed, dropped out, came back. Talk about rays! Then I asked them to close their mouths. Nothing. So now we begin with mouths open. Don't know if it qualifies as a "tiny Meeting," but it's working for us.

I realized that many of them were ashamed to laugh (more residue from judgment-heavy education?) I think they thought I would be mad at them. I have a new policy: always and under any circumstances laugh. Because if they live in fear of my judgment of their laughter, the whole relationship is off to a bad start. I need to <u>invite</u> their feelings. Laughter is usually the first feeling expressed. If we are in the business of helping people express themselves, stifling laughter is a bad way to begin. This group was very lively, and I'm certain that their liveliness, their ability to release emotionally into moments in their scenes, was rooted in the permission to laugh. Laughter is the first permissible feeling—you pass through it and other feelings await, repress it and none of them are available. I think spiritual searching can provoke laughter, like the way I wanted to laugh at Meetings at WFS. Laughter releases fear, which is the single greatest block ~~to creativity~~ to education that I can think of. They resisted the circle at first. It smacked of all the touchy-feely stuff Mamet objects, too. But as the class wore on, I think they even looked forward to it. It was an oasis from the noisiness of their other lives.

I skipped monologues and went straight to scenes, but I still felt like we took a giant step backwards then. We had been playing all these games and improv[19] exercises, getting loose, opening up, and then scene work began and they all froze. The expectant faces came back. They stared at me like it was the first class all over again, like we hadn't been working with each other for four weeks. Looking back it felt like I taught two classes: one with games and exercises and one with scenes. I need to fix that. Ideas?

When scene work began, I completely lost the students who weren't in the scene being worked on—the student audience. As I was giving notes, I would look around and see these glazed and stupefied faces. One woman even told me she wanted to do more exercises, that she wasn't learning anything from "all the talking." I was shocked. She might as well have said, "You talk too much." It's not my responsibility to entertain them while I teach, but on the other hand, I feel bad. The students watching are paying for that class, too. But I can't see more than two scenes in a class without short-changing the scenes that come in.

[19]Short for "improvisation."

I feel stuck, and it makes me completely paranoid when I give notes. I have this nightmare that I'll pause and suddenly realize that everyone has fallen asleep, except for the two I'm talking to.

Then there's the question of side-coaching. When do you butt in? I remember it used to drive me crazy when a teacher wouldn't let us get three lines out before stopping us to make an adjustment. Now as a teacher, these scenes come in filled with mistakes and unfulfilled moments and all I want to do is say "Stop! Go back!" But when I do, I can tell I've knocked them off the beam, and any momentum they had was lost. Worse, they begin to distrust their good instincts, and instead wait for me to tell them what to do, which only makes me more irritable. There must be some middle ground. I'm at my best when a scene is going well, and I find myself saying "Good!" out loud underneath moments which work.

Other news: I'm in a commercial for a toy called "Silly Soup," in which kids try to fish items out of a spinning bowl. I was supposed to play The Goofy Young Dad, which was all I had to go on as a description. So I put on this old striped blazer, a bow tie, a pair of nerdy character glasses and I freaked my hair out with some product. Apparently I overdid it. In the hallway, the casting agent was checking people in. When she looked at me she asked who I was auditioning for. I said "The Goofy Young Dad." She looked at me long and hard, then she said, "No. I think you're better for The Insane Person." I'm not making this up. So they cast me as The Insane Person.

In the ad, all hell breaks loose in a Goofy Diner when a boy orders some silly soup. I spin around on a lunch counter stool and shriek in my insane way: "Silly Soup! Silly Soup!" Did you ever see the movie "Finding Nemo?" Do you remember the fish in the tank that shouts "Bubbles! Bubbles!" when the treasure chest opens and bubbles? He was my source of inspiration. But a job's a job and the paycheck doesn't suck. This is how the game is played, right?

I'm also in an original play about the 9/11 attacks, called Dust. It's really powerful stuff: imagined scenes from inside the planes, inside the towers, and of observers. Interspersed with this gritty realism are these movement theater segments that use myths and legends about flying, war, grief, and re-birth as text. The piece tries to lift the attacks into a mythic realm where they can be witnessed and felt from a safe distance. It's performed in and around this big cage/jungle-gym, with ropes and pulleys that lift us into the air. It ends with me playing a little boy who's playing with airplanes, airplanes that knock over buildings. It's a very simple image and it's devastating. In my newly raw state, I can barely keep from falling apart on stage.

As you can imagine, this piece has become very meaningful to me. The group that wrote it and is producing it is called Moveable Feast, and we perform it in this tiny theater on the lower east side. Each night they have to put pillows on the floor in front of the first row to cram people in. Each night we, actors and audience, embark on this unified experience. They feel less like audience and more like partners. I catch myself watching them from the stage, and the looks of awe, of despair, of cathartic release stimulate that still, small voice inside. It says, Look, this is why it's good to be an actor.

Moveable Feast can barely pay my train fare, but I would walk barefoot from my apartment on 83rd street to do this play if I had too. This is what I want it to be like, always. How can I make that happen? And I wonder, why can't the theater bring us together the way Dust does all the time, without needing a catastrophe as a subject? Maybe it says something about the community I live in. What community? I see my community most clearly on the subway. Riding the A train, surrounded by the amazing quilt of cultures in this amazing city, from the immigrants to the hipsters and everyone in between, I think: it's you. You're who I'm doing this for. If only you would come. Why do I feel so disconnected from this city?

I've had to cut back on my restaurant shifts. TAG has offered me a "semi-permanent position" (what the hell does that mean?) as a teacher in their education program, and the opportunity to audition for all their shows. But they want me to take some workshops this summer. One of them is a Linklater[20] voice workshop, which I'd do even if I wasn't teaching. The Linklater work was a part of my training at Emerson and it's a kind of foundation for me. The other is an acting-teacher development program at Haverford College. So I may be coming back to your neck of the woods.

---

[20]Kristin Linklater, author of *Freeing the Natural Voice*, has an approach to actor vocal training named after her.

There's actually a "perfect storm" blowing me to you, Alice. I'm seeing this girl. She's in <u>Dust</u>. Her name is Maya Pelli and her family lives in Narberth, Pennsylvania. She set up a residency for Moveable Feast at The University of The Arts in July/August (her Dad works there). So we'll be working on <u>Dust</u> a few miles away from you before doing it at the Philly Fringe and, well, I'm smitten so I might just follow Maya around—at least for the summer. Visit my grandparents in Newtown Square. Maybe you and Sam and me and Maya could double date (how's it going with Sam?)

Maya and I will arrive just after Memorial Day. We'll stay with her parents. I'll call you and you'd better answer your phone! Won't it be cool to get together?

Love,
Andy

[script in black fountain pen on embossed stationery, "The Quad, Swarthmore, Pennsylvania" printed on the top of each page]

May 21st, 2005

Dear Andy,

Every now and then, we get a Divine message that comes through loud and clear. I think the one we're getting, you and I, is that God wants us to meet! So be it. Call when you and your lady friend arrive, and we will make plans.

I wish I could write that I am overjoyed that we will see each other, after all these years. But I have so loved our epistolary relationship, you must promise me that we shall continue writing to each other, even after we have met. We have been indulging in a lost art: the exchange of letters between two who miss each other. It used to be more common, and I have had several like this with various suitors. I love the time between letters, the way it intensifies longing. I love the tactile feel of the letters themselves, the hungry way I open their envelopes. I love the way they lie around my apartment, the way I linger with them and begin writing the response days before I pick up my pen. And I love my pen, I love its wet black mark on the yielding page, which soaks up something of me to send to you. I much preferred your handwritten letters, dear. I could sense the fury in your script, I could almost smell the path of your hand as it moved across the yellow page. Good letters should be sensual, don't digitize your sensuality with a keyboard. So you must keep writing to me, yes, even from Narberth. Chalk it up to an old woman's eccentricity.

You've asked me a great deal about teaching, and I will answer you, somehow, when I feel stronger. But let me at least attend to your personal queries. The simple answer to your first query is that I never met the right man. But the simple answer isn't always truthful. I think I never wanted to feel trapped, the way my mother was trapped. I had no good model of a marriage I liked, and I liked my independence too much. I came into adulthood in the sixties, when being unattached had its convenience. No horrible diseases were being passed around. Do I shock you? Most people can't imagine their teachers being sexual, my own stomach turns at the thought. And Quakers don't have sex at all, at least that's the perception. But I led a double life for many years: proper English/Drama teacher during the school year, single adult New York student-actor during the summers. Summers were for making art and whoopee.

Recently, I've felt regret for my independent choices. I pine for the fairy tale of romance and the perfect partner, the way you have pined for the fairy tale of fame. But what's the use? I am who I am. I did what I did. This is the bed I made, and I lie in it though it's lonely, especially at the end of my life. But at least it's familiar.

You see, it really is the end of my life. I'm dying, Andy. ~~Which is why part~~ why I didn't want to speak on the phone with you, ~~and why~~ I'm sorry. The distance is easier. And I didn't lie to you. I think I said phones are a nuisance, or something.

I have some kind of blood condition with a long name.[21] I get transfusions every other week, or so. I'm not making enough red blood cells to keep myself alive. In quaint "medi-speak" it's treatable, not curable. I'm often very weak and I suffer the indignity of a wheelchair from time to time. This gets to your second query. I haven't been painting an entirely realistic picture for you. I'm at The Quad because I need the medical care it provides, and my disdain for it is a kind of self-contempt. I hate myself for getting old, for having a disease, for dying. I don't want anyone to see me like this, it's embarrassing. This condition I have will eventually kill me. It's either here or a hospital. I wouldn't last a month on my own.

What creativity can there be when you're waiting to die? I have fun with Edith. And Sam, the pest, keeps me entertained in his way. But what project is worth embarking on when one isn't sure one will see the fall? Sometimes in the summer they leave windows open on the third floor hallways and I have terrible thoughts. All this honesty is tiring me more quickly than usual. I'm afraid I don't have it in me to write you your usual novella.

I did read the Mamet and the Bates, though. Any book that makes you throw it across the room is a valuable book, a visceral reaction is always better than ambivalence, and Mamet has done us a service by asking us to look hard at what we do when we teach acting. And yet, I fear his hubris is swollen and someone should lance it. He speaks plainly though, and that appeals to my Quaker sensibilities. So much of the current discussion about actor training is couched in thick, jargon-laden post-modern speak, especially in the Journals of Higher Whatever. But he's made the common mistake of confusing Stanislavsky with "The Method," a term which has no meaning any longer. I liked the chapter called "Habit." By the way, did you know he is a

---

[21]Alice had Myelodysplastic disorder, a degenerative blood condition that in her case led to leukemia.

Meisner protégé of sorts? He spent a year immersed in the Repetition exercises, which explains some of his plays.[22]

Bates, as I suspected, is my spirit-brother, and his words about the actor's source of power should be taken to heart. But he gets too charmed by the famous people he interviews. I wish he had interviewed run of the mill actors. Damn it, why didn't someone do a survey about us?

Oh Andy. I have so much to say to you and I suddenly feel the great shadow upon me. Now I can't wait to see you. Get here quickly, please, and show me how to make something out of these final moments. Endings are the hardest to write. ~~I need~~ I'm all over the place. I need someone to hold me.

Love,
Alice

PS: Who is Bill Wilson? A teacher of yours?

---

[22]Mamet studied with Bill Esper, a student of Meisner's and the major teacher of his technique. Repetition is a standard Meisner exercise, in which actors repeat observations of each other back and forth, leading to a more unselfconscious use of language. Alice's joke is that Mamet's dialogue occasionally has a staccato, repetitive quality reminiscent of this exercise.

[printed script in red felt-tip pen on yellow legal pad]

May 23

Dear Alice,

I went to a Meeting as well as a meeting yesterday. Maya came too. I felt so lost about what's happening to you, so sad. I felt like this would be a way to honor you. We sat in Stuyvesant Square Park for a half hour, just watching the morning come, then we went inside the Meeting room. I had some melodramatic expectation—that I would arrive and just cry.

But instead, an extraordinary calm and clarity came over me in the stillness of meeting for worship. I had a vision. First I saw you sitting in the room with me. You were as you were 13 years ago: slender and mysterious. You had a distant look on your face, then you looked at me. The vision expanded and I saw you at The Quad making theater. I saw myself at your side. I saw myself at the teaching workshop at Haverford College, with you in the corner watching me, taking notes. I saw us on stage together in <u>Dust</u>. My still, small voice said, "You will make this happen." A burning urgency has alighted inside me, Alice. I need so badly now to become ~~what I want to~~ what I am becoming. I need you closer to guide me.

I thought of you and the loves in your life. Instead of feeling embarrassed, I felt inspired. I imagined you as Juliet. Then I imagined you as Juliet as you are today at 72. Then I imagined making a piece of theater with the elderly at The Quad, using <u>Romeo and Juliet</u> as a starting point. All this from the stillness of that great room and the people gathered there.

Then a woman rose and spoke. She spoke of being at a crossroads, in which she knew she would have to make a choice, but she still wasn't sure what that choice was. She spoke of faith as being the opposite of fear. She mentioned the Frost poem about the road not taken. She ended by saying that moving into this new phase in her life was scary, but she felt immense gratitude for the love of those gathered around her. I felt electricity shooting up and down my back, I was a little dizzy, I lost my breath. I thought she had read my mind.

IT HAD TO DO WITH HER PARTNER, I THINK.

Here's the facts. Maya and I arrive this weekend. We will be staying in Narberth with her parents, and she said we'll be able to borrow their car. So I will call you, you will answer your phone, and we will make plans. You see, I don't care about your disease. Or I only care about it because it puts you in pain, but I will not let it hold us back. We will go forward into the future together gently, and not ask how much time we have left, but only what do we feel like doing today. Because today is all we have.

I want to witness that beautiful bird take flight again.

Love,
Andy

❧

Summer

STUDY

During the summer of 2005, Alice and Andy worked together on a special project at the Quad with a variety of friends, and Alice observed Andy at the Acting Teacher's Workshop at Haverford College. Included in this section are a broader assortment of documents: handouts from the workshop, Alice's observations of the workshop and Andy's rehearsal notes, for example. The letters include some new voices, a trend which continues in the final section. During this summer, Andy kept his promise to keep writing letters, even though he was living only a half an hour away.

—L.E.B.

[The following was handed out to the Haverford College Acting Teacher Workshop participants on the first day by Assistant Professor of Theatre Barbara Lewis]

The Four-Fold Way[23]

To Cultivate:

The Four-Fold Way
1. Show Up and Be Present
2. Pay Attention to what has Heart and Meaning
3. Tell the Truth without Judgment or Blame
4. Be Open to Outcome, but not Attached to Outcome

To Avoid:

The Underlying Addictions
Addiction to Intensity
Addiction to the Myth of Perfection
Addiction to Focusing on What's Not Working
Addiction to Having to Know

---

[23]Arrien, Angeles. *The Four-Fold Way* (1993: Harper Collins, San Francisco). Note: the words "the Myth of" in The Myth of Perfection are Ms. Lewis's addition.

[Alice's first workshop observation, pencil on white, lined notebook pages]

June 8th, 2005

Since you told me Miss Lewis won't mind, I'll share these notes with you later. Still feels a little sneaky, though. Can't make heads or tails of this ~~4~~Four-Fold Way business. I'll look at it more closely when I get home. She calls it a framework for investigation. ~~Investigating what? It seems more like~~

Yes, she addresses your concern about serving the entire class, each class. You must <u>invite</u> feedback. This is how those who are not performing learn. But take care not to judge the feedback, unless the feedback itself is judgmental. The beginning student barely understands what he's seeing. We learn about acting by doing it, and by trying to speak about it. Your job is to give the class a non-judgmental vocabulary to articulate what they see and experience. And the vocabulary must be <u>consistent</u>.

And you must define the <u>context</u>. There should never be a class called "Beginning Acting" or "Principles of Acting." What kind of acting? Who's principles? Remember: what we call acting generally in this country is a very new <u>style</u> of acting called realism.

Miss Lewis is talking about indicating[24] now and how it should be avoided. But indicating is perfectly fine in farce, in melodrama, even in some musicals. Call it "Basic Realism," or, if you want to teach "Basic Acting," then teach it over the course of a year and leave room for non-realistic styles.

This woman is breaking her own rule—a frequent problem with acting teachers. We say, "Be concise, strive for clarity," and then we go on and on and on. Strasberg[25] was famous for this. I haven't heard a word she's said for the last five minutes. With Miss Lewis

---

[24]Indicating means the artificial representation of emotions through gestures and facial expressions.

[25]Lee Strasberg, Group Theatre leader and founder of The Actors Studio. He is generally agreed to be the father of what became known as "Method" acting.

---

this is an aspect of insecurity—she is afraid she isn't up to helping all you young teachers so she is "padding." She isn't embracing her role as Mom, she's not yet comfortable with that authority. Because the sound of her own voice comforts her, and your expectant faces scare her, she stays in her own solipsistic loop. Oops, she just saw me scribbling away and lost her place. Good, we're moving on.

I think she wants to be your peer as well as your teacher. Impossible. A peer is your equal, a teacher is not, though she can be friendly. This is tricky, and the requisite balancing act is learned only after years of experience. She just needs to relax and trust herself more. Students need the teacher to have and demonstrate authority, but that doesn't mean you have to be a minaret. The authority's only purpose is to make the students feel safe to explore and risk. It is the benevolent authority of the parent.

Students are leading exercises now. ~~I don't get the~~ The Asian woman is leading the Red Square exercise. Fascinating. Very Quaker.[26]

Now you're leading The Grid.[27] I like it, but let me throw in a word about exercises—and this speaks to your concern about your NYC class having "two parts," one for exercises, one for scenes. I used to think exercises could stand on their own as a valuable part of my students' instruction. But I came to believe that exercises are only valuable if the teacher can connect them to the overall curriculum in a meaningful way. ~~The students need they~~ Students don't need to know why they are doing an exercise <u>before</u> they do it—indeed, exploring without knowing is a critical part of the actor's training. But <u>afterwards</u>, the teacher should draw a line between the exercise and a larger purpose. Or better yet, when a student makes creative physical choices in a scene, teacher should draw the line <u>backwards</u> to the Grid. The student will seldom make these connections on his own, and most acting students need structure and context to feel safe. Provide that context after the exercise. This will invite feedback as well.

---

[26]The Red Square is described in the appendix.

[27]The Grid is described in the appendix.

I have always felt that acting classes should begin with a kind of "boot camp"—to borrow a dreadful military term. But in the same way the armed forces build "unit cohesion" or whatever they call it, so too should an acting class build an ensemble straight away. These exercises you are sharing with each other now and all the games you learned from me are excellent ways to bring a class of shy young people together by spreading the embarrassment around and making it fun. They also address some important fundamentals, like getting students out of their heads and using their bodies creatively. Miss Lewis is suggesting that you release your anxiety into these exercises, yes, that is what acting class boot camp is for. In a semester, three weeks of this or so, then short scenes, then long scenes.

But some teachers get lost in their own exercises. Students take an acting class to learn to act. Call me old-fashioned, but to me that means performing dramatic language. It means acting in scenes. The sooner you get to scene work, the better, and the more excited the students will be. It's what they came for! This is not to say that exercises have no value, or should be skipped—but be sure you can point out the ways they are leading to expressive acting in scenes.

Unless acting in scenes is <u>not</u> what "acting" means to you. But if that's so, you better be sure the students know what acting <u>does</u> mean to you at the outset, otherwise you may be accused of selling a phony bill of goods down the line. Again, what kind of acting are you teaching?

Damn you for dragging me into The Grid. In my wheelchair no less! I'll get you for this, Andy Fallon!

That was invigorating.

But no one offered exercises with physical touching. And I thought you were all so "free!" This is an essential barrier to cross early. And of course I don't mean anything sexual, my God we've gotten so scared of human contact in the arts because of the perverse stories we've all heard. We used to give each other massages in some of the classes I took, and then lie all over each other while we watched each other work. Perfectly innocent! But that innocence has been lost, and we live in fear of human contact now, a trend which must be reversed. Do you remember that Grouping exercise I did with all of you, in which I asked each student to take the others by the hand and group them in ways that seemed appropriate?[28] It wasn't the <u>grouping</u> that I was after, it was the <u>holding hands</u> and pulling around the room! The Remembering Hands[29] exercise is another one. Make them touch each other—safely.

Now Miss Lewis is modeling excellent teaching. She is leading a discussion about the exercises you've all just done, but she is disguising any agenda or point of view. I can see the students squirming, trying to figure out a response to what you've all just done together, having to formulate observations without knowing what Miss Lewis is looking for. As usual, the initial responses are over-the-top generous and supportive. Good. The ensemble is being built and nothing wrong with being jolly to begin. Now she asks some pointed questions, and she asks that you all speak without "judgment or blame"—interesting phrase. She asks you to ask questions of each other. She is guiding your criticism. Excellent.

Here we go. A young man is getting defensive. Some of you didn't like his exercise. She jumps in. She questions the questioners. What exactly didn't you like? What might that say about you? Now it's a chat about how each class will reflect the tastes and sensibilities of each teacher. Yes. But I would add, this is why you must spend your life continually asking, what does this class mean to me? What am I giving to my students?

---

[28]Grouping is described in the appendix.

[29]Remembering Hands is described in the appendix.

[typed in courier font, "Haverford College, Department of Fine & Performing Arts" embossed on the top of each page]

June 12

Dear Ms. Jones,

I'm happy to respond to your question. It's been fine having you in class. Please don't worry about being a distraction. If there's ever a problem I'll let you know. You add a kind of dignity to the proceedings, I think!

The Four-Fold Way is a book by Dr. Angeles Arrien, which on the surface has nothing to with acting. I have culled some of the seminal ideas in the book and use them as guides in my classes. The book is an investigation of the belief systems of tribal peoples in the world, and an attempt to articulate those beliefs in a way that might help a modern person. It came to me through a conference on Theater and Multiculturalism I attended. I was instantly struck by how applicable these eight ideas are to an actor's experience, especially the student actor.

"Show Up and Be Present." I love the distinction between just showing up—what so many students do in an attempt to glide through their education—and being present, what the acting class demands. I also love that it doesn't say, "Show Up and Be Happy."

"Pay Attention to What Has Heart and Meaning." Isn't this what the actor is called to do? What are we searching for in a character, unless we search for that aspect of the character that calls to us in some way. We had a robust discussion about this in one of the classes you missed. Martin asked about evil characters. How can we search Iago for what has heart and meaning? Or if we are cast as Hitler? I said that in that case the heart and meaning must be found in the play itself. We cannot play Iago without believing in the message of Othello. This led to a discussion about leading full lives as artists, that we seek what has heart and meaning in everything we do. Ed chimed in, what about when you just need to pay the rent? And we agreed—we are speaking of an ideal, an ideal that has to be tempered by the realities of paying bills. Andy offered that heart and meaning can be found in a good comedy. What can be more important than making people laugh in a world that is so full of tension and sadness? This idea also helps describe what the student actor looks for when watching his peers.

"Tell the Truth Without Judgment or Blame." This gets to the challenge of speaking honestly about each other's work. Wei Li brought up tact. Most agreed that there is a time and place for "rigorous honesty." We are teaching our students to trust what they see, and respond to it truthfully. Expressing a response without judgment or blame shifts the focus away from the actor in question, and on to the event witnessed. What did you see, or not see, and how did you respond to it? If we need to be critical, we can tell the truth without the message being that someone *is bad*. The message instead is that I think you could *do it* better. This distinction is crucial in actor training, in which criticism can so easily be taken personally. Andy spoke about the Quaker Testimony of Integrity—something he learned from you?

"Be Open to Outcome, but Not Attached to Outcome." The student actor wants to do well, and so will try to control the outcome of the exercise, improvisation, or scene they're in. This will inevitably shut down exploration and creativity. Worse, it negates the possibility of their partner adding anything to the event. This phrase speaks to the essence of collaboration—we have to be open to what comes our way, even as we pursue our purpose in the scene.

"The Underlying Addictions." Isn't this a list of modern neuroses, with special application to the theater?

"The Addiction to Intensity." What every shouting actor or drama queen demonstrates. It speaks to the tendency for beginning actors to attempt to manufacture "drama," because they haven't learned to trust the power of genuine living in given circumstances.[30]

"The Addiction to Focusing on What's Not Working." Focusing on what's not working is a recipe for creative paralysis. This is a warning against the perils of frustration, and obsession with "mistakes." I encourage them to flip it around and focus on what *is* working. These have also seemed to me to be wise words for the teacher, whose job I think is to highlight what the student does *well*, more than criticize what the student does poorly.

"The Addiction to Having to Know." This is an invitation for each student to work without being sure what the outcome will be. It's also a way to de-emphasize the "logic centers" of the brain, so cultivated in college. It's a way to invite learning from somewhere else besides the frontal lobe.

"The Addiction to the Myth of Perfection." Perfection is impossible, unattainable and detrimental to the actor. So many of us want to get it "right." I tell my students there is no such thing in my class. But there is also no such

---

[30] "Given circumstances" is a phrase that generally means the fictional world of the play, especially the physical and psychological condition of the character.

---

thing as "wrong." There are only choices, some are more effective than others, which is where I come in. And anyway, aren't the imperfections what make life interesting?

I hope this clears up the Four-Fold Way a bit. At the end of the workshop, I will assign a paper (more of a journaling exercise, really) and ask each student to connect some of their own experience with these ideas. I'm not surprised these ideas seem unusual to you. It's been a bit of a struggle getting my department to acknowledge the usefulness of investigations that seem to lack intellectual "value." But more and more, I'm feeling that acting and the teaching of it *isn't* intellectual in nature, and is full of aspects that are hard to describe. The Four-Fold Way gives me a framework for those aspects.

On an unrelated topic, Andy spoke movingly about you the first day of the workshop. I asked the students to describe an interesting recent event in their lives as a way to get to know each other, and he spoke of your re-appearance in his life. He got quite emotional, actually. I understand that you have a great deal of experience teaching acting, and have done so at the college level (do I have this right?) Anyway, I am applying for tenure next year and am feeling a bit frantic about it. I'm worried that if I present the ideas that are truly mean-ingful to me in my application, I'm doomed! If you have the time, and have anything to say about it, I'd be most grateful.

See you in class soon, I hope!

Your friend,
Barbara Lewis

[printed script in blue ballpoint pen on stationery, "From the desk of Dr. Ian Pelli, 529 Windsor Ave, Narberth, PA" printed on each page]

6/14/05

Dear Alice,

Thanks for the notes from class. I'm saving everything and re-reading a lot of stuff you write. I need time to digest it all!

It's been so wonderful to see you again, after all these years. But strange too. I was so grateful when you answered the phone a couple of weeks ago, but I was unprepared at how awkward I felt. In addition to the Alice of my memory (the Magical Mom the with the long hair, baggy pants, and batik shirts) I realized that I had created yet another "Alice"—the Alice of your letters. You were this Goddess to me in these last tumultuous months, visiting me out of the ether with ~~these words from on~~ divine missives. You might as well have been a benevolent Oz. What a shock to hear your sweet, shy voice on the phone, and then to see you, walking carefully down the hall to me and Maya, dressed in that dazzling Indian wrap, silver-white hair in wound-up braids on your head, holding the rail every now and then to steady yourself, bright green eyes as piercing as ever.

You have lost none of your eccentric beauty. You still sparkle. You are still full of mischief, and when I'm with you, all I want to do is ~~run away with~~ get into trouble with you. And my God you have nothing to be ashamed of. It makes me so mad that old people are made to feel this way by a culture that regards the natural process of aging as a curse, rather than the difficult ripening and letting go that it is. When did we lose our reverence for elders? I think of other cultures in which the grandparents are taken into the home and cared for. Maya grew up with "Nona," her name for her father's mother, living in a room downstairs. Maya had a very strong reaction to The Quad—as polished and well equipped as it is. She called it a "ghetto." Then we had an argument.

You see, I know that you need to be there. And I'm not willing to condemn assisted living categorically. But I think there is a way for you to do something there that will feed you artistically (you know where this is going, don't you). I know you hate the <u>Romeo and Juliet</u> idea, but I'm asking one more time: let me organize a reading there. That's all. Just a reading, and if you and Edith and Sam and the rest of your friends all look at me like I'm crazy afterwards then, well, at least we read a great play together out loud. Not a bad way to spend the evening, right?

Maya and I will pick you and Edith up Friday at 5:00. Dinner and a play. See you at Haverford this week, too?

Love,
Andy

[Alice's workshop observation, pencil on white, lined notebook pages]

June 17, 2005

Martin is giving you and Wei Li notes on your <u>Fool For Love</u> scene. He makes the critical error of remaining in his chair, which is in the middle of the line of chairs that the students are sitting in, against the wall, facing you and your partner. He is talking too much and losing us all. Why doesn't Miss Lewis interrupt him?

And why don't you applaud for each other after the scenes? Not applauding seems like a criticism. Actors act in part for the applause, so let them have it—plus, it builds the ensemble.

After the scene is finished, Teacher should create a triangle [*the following was drawn by Alice in her notebook*]:

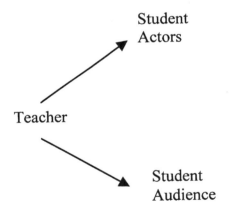

This is the right relationship when giving notes and encouraging feedback. You are facilitating a conversation, you can keep an eye on the whole class, you can call on a particular student, you can filter inappropriate feedback. Most of all, you are demonstrating that this is a learning experience for everyone, not

THE ACTOR'S WAY

only the ones who have just performed. Everyone pays for every class; everyone should be instructed in every class.

Miss Lewis is addressing you now, and referring to a moment I barely remember. By the way, I think you overplayed Eddie's rage with May. He's a cowboy—rampaging about the room diminishes him. May throws herself about the room, which Wei Li did quite well. She's good. Miss Lewis should tell you that you succumbed to your addiction to intensity.

But that was 15 minutes ago now and the moment's been lost. The acting teacher needs to seize the moment of the actor's discovery—seize it and freeze it—just for a moment—and point it out to the actor and to the class. It is the immediacy of the actor's discoveries that make them so hard to comprehend. But this is our challenge, to be so "present" (to use your new favorite word) that we can leap at the student's success, or mistake, and point it out.

Now to contradict myself: the first time in, I like to let the scene play through once without stopping. I think they deserve to be able to show the result of their work in its entirety. This way, the student actors get to show us the totality of their choices first, they get to release their nervous energy into the scene unimpeded by Teacher, and we have a complete canvas to which we can respond. Then brief, focused feedback. I make sure to ask the actors themselves for feedback first. If they both thought it went terribly, I should know that. I try to draw the students' attention to something that caught my eye—either a problem or a success—without being too explicit. I want the student audience to struggle to articulate a response. Then the student actors perform it again. It is during this work-through that I seize and freeze, and also side-coach.

The Long Day's scene is up now. Not going so well. Why is she giving you these old ~~chestnuts~~ plays with middle-aged characters? The oldest of you is twenty-something? How can you possibly relate to Vanya's mid-life crisis, or Tyrone's despair? And the scenes are too long. 15 % of total time is my equation. If I have 60 minutes for a pair of students working on a scene, then that scene should run no longer than 9 minutes. 30 minutes for a pair equals a 5 minute scene—roughly. I studied with a Russian once who assigned me and a partner a page of dialogue between Masha and Kulygin from Three Sisters. One page. A minute total. We spent hours on this tiny bit—agony, and enlightenment. And I was 32—the right age to be working on Masha.

Back to side-coaching. Knew another teacher who aggressively side-coached. I was playing Amanda in Glass Menagerie. During my scene with Tom, this teacher strutted about shouting "You hate him Alice! He's a little faggot! You want to kill him!" It was so awful I eventually burst into tears towards the end of the scene. The class was impressed, the teacher regarded it as an Important Breakthrough. "You see, I speak to your subconscious," he said later. Rubbish. I cried because he was yelling at me while I was trying to act. I never came back. Whisper to me while I sleep if you want to speak to my subconscious. What this man was doing was pedagogical assault and battery.

Side-coaching is only useful as encouragement. You nudge the student. You wrote about your little murmurs of "Good!" while teaching—dead on. You're basically cheering the actor on when she's getting it right (you see my dear, there is right and wrong, unpleasant though you may find it).[31] When I do my work-throughs, I side-coach the good bits, and I stop the scene when it veers in the wrong direction, otherwise bad habits are left uncorrected.

There is an advanced form of side-coaching, only to be employed between students and teachers who have worked together for a while, and only when the student knows before they start that it's coming. It's simply a more aggressive kind of encouragement, the way a coach might shout at a player during a practice. But when to shout and what to say requires teachers of great discretion and students of some experience. If I used names, I used the characters' names, never employed foul language, and the gist of it was always a variation of "Come on! You can do this!"

My, my, this Joslyn likes to talk, too! Some teachers are frustrated actors, and so teaching becomes their performance. There is a vital connection between teaching and performing and we should celebrate it. It's fun. But when teaching becomes a substitute for acting, we're in trouble. Any teacher in the arts should practice the art they teach. Nothing worse than a bitter actor who settles for teaching—and universities are full of them. Glad to hear Miss Lewis is an active Equity[32] actor. This is another reason why student feedback is so important. It

[31]Alice seems to refer to something Barbara Lewis wrote here, not something Andy wrote.
[32]Refers to Actors Equity Association, the union of professional stage actors.

prevents the teacher from monopolizing the experience. You just made the "throat slashing" gesture to me. Am I scribbling too loudly?

Ah! Miss Lewis said it! To the whole class, she said: "You're all talking too much!" I would have said it ten minutes ago, but it's not my class, is it?

[script in black fountain pen on embossed stationery, "The Quad, Swarthmore, Pennsylvania" printed on the top of each page]

June 18th, 2005

Dear Miss Lewis,

Thanks you for your kind reply to my inquiry about <u>The Four-Fold Way</u>. While I remain skeptical about contributions to the field of acting from conferences on "multiculturalism," I have come to admire these ideas and the way you are employing them. Maybe I'm just old-fashioned. I appreciate the way you weave them into your feedback on work brought into class, just enough so that the ideas stay "present" as you are fond of saying. Your students see the ideas at work, which is the only way they are useful.

I had not grasped them as spiritual ideas at first, but now I understand that that is what they are. In presenting them to your class you are indeed breaking new ground (or re-breaking old ground) nevermind. My advice about them as pedagogical tools is that you frame them as <u>spiritual</u> ideas. You mustn't apologize for them, nor feel the urge to justify them intellectually. If you believe that spiritual ideas have import for an acting class, then you must find the courage to share them as such. But be prepared for a lively discussion, and deep skepticism from the university. It's a pity you feel resistance to this investigation from your department. Haverford College was ostensibly founded on spiritual principles—ones that I am a follower of, in fact. If you are not too busy, I would be glad to speak with you about those principles some day, face to face. Discussions about spiritual matters are best done in person.

I will now speak to your concern about your tenure application, but with great trepidation. You should know that after I graduated from Swarthmore, I received a PhD. in Theatre from the University of Massachusetts in 1969. Needing to be close to my mother who was in ill health and living in Germantown, Pennsylvania, I received a tenure-track position teaching acting and theater history at a nearby university, which shall remain nameless—nameless because I buried that hatchet long ago.

I taught a variety of graduate and undergraduate classes and participated in the requisite departmental committee meetings. I brought many guest artists and teachers to the university to give workshops and teach summer classes. I initiated a study-abroad program in theater which later foundered, this university not having a vibrant enough cultural life to generate the necessary student numbers, and because of my inability to draw together students from other colleges. I tried to get on university committees and failed repeatedly, my gender and status as a teacher of acting putting me at a disadvantage. And, most importantly for me anyway, I acted during the summers.

In my application for tenure, I held up my work as an actor as analogous to scholarly publications. I had written nothing. I had nothing to say since I was in the process of discovering who I was as a teacher, what worked for me, what didn't. But the discoveries I made during the summers I acted I brought back into the classroom and shared with my students. There was always a dynamic relationship between my acting and my teaching. Indeed, looking back, I see now I could never have done one without the other.

I was denied tenure, the university stating, to my surprise, that my creative work was commendable (apparently they bought the equation of actorly work to publication—forward-looking for a conservative university in the mid-seventies), but said my teaching and service were inadequate.[33] My surprise came mostly from the fact that during my six years there, no one from the university had ever come to watch me teach, and my student evaluations during my last four years were equal to or better than my department's in most categories. I called the chair of my department and asked if I could depend upon the support of the department if I launched an appeal. He said I could not. I put down the phone and cried.

I imagine you are asking yourself, why is she telling me all this? I speak to you of my experience, which is all I have. But I have shared my story with others in universities who say it is not an unusual one. Universities make a great to-do about how these decisions are impersonal and unbiased, when frequently, exactly the reverse is the truth. When I hung up the phone that day I knew my denial of tenure had nothing to do with what kind of teacher I was. How could it, since no one had watched me teach? And since the university apparently supported my creative work, I was left with only one answer: The people I worked with didn't like me, or I made them uncomfortable—couch it any way you want. They didn't want me there, with them, and that's why I was denied tenure. The decision was based on aspects of my personality, aspects that in my thirties were set, based as they were and are in core of who I am: as an artist, a

---

[33]Tenure applications are usually divided into three main categories: research (in Alice's case artistic work), teaching, and service.

Quaker, a woman, a human being. To have pretended to be someone else in order to gain the favor of the people I was working with would have been a kind of spiritual suicide.

I was granted the usual "lame duck" year after I was denied tenure. Even more wounding than the university's decision was the silence I received from my former colleagues. No one had the time or courage to have the difficult encounter with me about why things turned out as they had. My department chair told me to "read my file"[34] if I wanted to understand the decision. My one overt act of defiance, and it was a pitiful one, was that I never read that file, feeling that without having seen me work in the classroom, my colleagues could have written nothing useful in it for me to read. Looking back, I see that I wanted to force a human encounter with them, a kind of discussion in which people seek not to explain logically, but to unburden emotionally. It is an encounter of the heart, not the mind. These encounters need to be demonstrably bound in love, and their fuel is courage. But this kind of encounter is anathema to most universities, which, in my experience, are conflict-averse places populated with intellectually snobbish cowards. That my longed-for encounter never happened confirms for me both the fraudulence of that tenure decision, as well as my colleagues' shame working in the shadow of it that final year. For what, after all, could they have said to me? What love could hold such an encounter in safety? And so we slunk through the hallways past each other, exchanging fixed smiles, the commerce of "collegiality" in the halls of academe.

Well, maybe that hatchet wasn't buried quite as deeply as I had hoped. Miss Lewis, I must stress to you, this is what happened to me. Something wonderful may happen to you. The way these decisions are handled reflects the character of the institutions which make them. My sense of Haverford is much more positive than my memory of that other place, and I hope that university culture has evolved over the last 30 years. The mere fact that your workshop has been so supported by the college is a very good sign indeed. My advice for you? Since you are applying next fall, there is little to change in your approach. Polonius said it best: "This above all: to your own self be true." You must present Haverford with the ideas that are truly meaningful to you. They are who you are.

---

[34]Alice refers to her tenure file, containing the commentary of departmental and university committees, which presumably would explain how they reached their judgements.

THE ACTOR'S WAY

Anything less would be dishonest and a violation of your life's work. Write what you believe, then let the chips fall where they may. If it ends badly, at least you will have integrity.

And it should be stated that something wonderful happened to me, after all. I began teaching at The Wallingford Friends' School the year after I was denied tenure. It turned out to be the ideal job for me, and afforded me the kind of freedom a university position might not have. I taught wonderful young people, and made lasting friendships with my colleagues working in an institution founded in my faith. I continued to act, and though the year or two around the tenure decision was hellish, the world didn't end. Way opened in a different way than I expected, which is the way it usually opens.

Thank you for letting me observe. Having been out of the classroom for some time now, I am finding it exhilarating, and exhausting! And I love writing and receiving letters, can you tell? I imagine Andy told you this was my preferred mode of communication. What do you think of him? He's swept into my life and lifted me off my feet in a most surprising way. I'm very fond of him. I'd love to hear your insights about him, and about teaching acting generally.

Your sister in Art,
Alice Jones

PS: Would you mind sending me a handwritten letter next time?

NOTES   6/20/05

Fight in beginning. Old men fighting? Comedy? All of which choose?
    Young/Old Capulet calls for sword — no good.
    Young Prince scolding old men — GREAT

Old Benvolio/Romeo better than expected if remembering something
    from long ago.

Nurse as young woman w/old Juliet — doesn't work, too big.
    But Maya's funny. Too biased — Seen it somehow?

Alice as Juliet — beautiful. Must talk to her about this idea
    of being the "right age" to work on a role.

Ennio as Mercutio, big surprise! Real simple even, Mob Scene. SAD

Maybe the whole thing _____ _____ — present it as
    an exper_____

R & J first _____ _____
    otherwise

Everyone's crying. Mak_____
    this is what I saw_____
    is it the final se_____

Part/Scene — from Lawrence/Ro_____
    like some kid & for Jue_____

Does it make fun of old people & then express? Is it
    patronizing?

II, iv, is a riot, with old two Kenzos, Mae & Benvolio making
    lewd jokes about young men. Maya's crying up

[Fight scene — could imitate the comedy of the gang, how to
    be by. Subtly horrible inability than we slowly get
    awkwardly towards murder? The shame of it
    brought right to the fore. Could be GHASTLY — in
    a GOOD way.

More crying, Alice barely made it through gallery scene.
And when he shall die, take him and cut in little stars —
the juxtaposition. Both, her age and the passion of the
speech is devastating — you sense the whole of the
and lives, and the closeness of her leaving through. Hot
comedy has whole new meaning. It's almost too much.
Alice make it work. She walked into it like an open
wound and waded through it, slowly, painfully, beautifully.
But SHE'S BEAMING now.

And to put it down in A.M. IV. People think. Clear we can't do
the whole thing — if we do anything at all.
Wonderful discussion about _____ _____ _____
elders. Some scuffled talk about _____ and love and loss. Maybe
this discussion is the additional material: MY crowd enthusiastic.
All agree it ought to be a new piece about _____ was
something about time into it. Jade, Rudy need to save this, for age
purpose, not other way around. MS will do a cutting and refine in two weeks.
Alice is staring at me with a mysterious smile.

[Andy's *Romeo and Juliet* notes, from a reading and discussion at the Quad. In attendance were Alice and several elderly friends, and Andy and Maya and some of their younger friends from Moveable Feast Theatre Company. Andy had older people reading younger roles, and vice versa. Blue ballpoint pen on yellow legal pad]

6/20/05

Fight in beginning. Old men fighting? Comedy? All in wheel-chairs? Young Old Capulet calling for crutch no good. Young Prince scolding old men is great.

Old Benvolio/Romeo better then expected. As if remembering something from long ago.

Nurse as young woman with old Juliet doesn't work straight up. But Maya's funny. But I'm biased. Spin it somehow?

Alice as Juliet—beautiful. Must talk to her about this idea of being the "right age" to work on a role.

Ernie as Mercutio big surprise! Real simple Queen Mab. Some-how sad.

Maybe the whole thing needs a "meta-frame"—present it as an experiment at a nursing home?

R & J first encounter end of act I touching, but we're dragging otherwise.

Everyone's crying. Balcony scene between Alice and Sam unbelievable. This is what I saw at NYC Quaker Meeting. This is the centerpiece, or is it the final scene? Construct something that ends w/this?

Dave/Sam—Friar Laurence/Romeo—funny! Makes this old man Romeo sound like some kind of Don Juan. Dave as Young Friar somehow just right.

Does it make fun of old people at their expense? Is it patronizing?

II, iv is a riot, with the old trio Romeo, Merc. & Benvolio making lewd jokes about young Nurse. Maya's cracking up.

Fight scene—can't imitate the comedy of opening. How to trans-late the violence realistically for old men? Can't be big. Something horrible in watching them move slowly and awkwardly towards murder? The shame of it brought right to the fore. Could be ghastly in a good way.

More crying. Alice barely made it through gallop apace. And when he shall die take him and cut in little stars—the juxtaposition btw. her age and the passion of the speech is devastating—you sense the whole of her life and loves, and the closeness of her leaving them. Night coming has whole new meaning. It's almost too much. Alice makes it work. She walked into it like an open wound and waded through it, slowly, painfully, beautifully. But she's beaming now.

Had to put it down in act IV. People tired. Clear we can't do the whole thing—if we do anything at all.

Wonderful discussion about what this unlocked for the elders. Some soulful talk about aging and love and loss. Maybe this discussion is the additional material? MF[35] crowd enthusiastic. All agree it needs to be a new piece that weaves something present-tense into R&J. Jack: R&J needs to serve the larger purpose, not other way around. MF will do a cutting and return in two weeks.

Alice is staring at me with a mysterious smile.

[script in black fountain pen on embossed stationery, "The Quad, Swarthmore, Pennsylvania" printed on the top of each page]

June 25th, 2005

Dear Andy,

I apologize for my part in our fight last Friday. You have to understand that you are pushing me into a situation that is fraught with danger for me. I have gotten used to a life in which I am an observer. You are asking me to be an actor again after all these years. Do you think that the fears all actors feel wane as you age? Quite the opposite: I'm far more frail than I was even two years ago, my memory's going and I look like a pale prune. And you're asking me to play Juliet! Not only that, but to somehow reveal, artistically, the anguish experience of aging in the first-person on stage. You should expect me to be a little prickly.

I am slowly coming around to your position. I can see the genesis of something interesting developing. I like these pups, these Feast people you've brought into the mix (although they dress like aborigines). And after all, it is Juliet, and I never played her when I should have, and there is something exciting about it. And who knew Sam could act?

But be prepared, young man, for a choppy sea as we sail forward together. Your kindness and open soul, the qualities I mentioned all those months ago when I was suggesting that you would make a good teacher, will also make you a good director. But a good director understands that when he asks an actor to be vulnerable in rehearsal, he shouldn't expect Emily Post during breaks. There's a stifling syndrome I call Enforced Cheerfulness, in which the one in charge demands smiles and a cheery disposition no matter the matter at hand. If the matter at hand involves great emotional risk, as does this journey for me, or psychic exhaustion of any kind, that experience will likely bleed into the actor's behavior outside the scene. We are not robots who switch from profound emotional exploration to giggles and backslaps at the flip of a switch, nor is the rehearsal room a place to expect people to "behave themselves," especially when the territory is dangerous. Enforced Cheerfulness is the worst kind of emotional dishonesty, which places a director's insecure need for false displays of "contentment" above the authentic experience of the person in question. It is an attempt to rig emotional control in a rehearsal and it is deadly. We are in the business of exploring and performing authentic experiences, and we should respect them—in and out of the scene. An actor faced with a great psychological challenge will exhibit any number of bizarre and often negative reactions to her fear of that challenge. Your job, if you're going to direct, is to support her, not scold her about her attitude.

A good rehearsal room has padded walls and a mat on the floor, sometimes actually and always metaphorically. The padded walls will take whatever the actor gives, they will keep the room soundproof and private, they will ensure no harm comes from the great release. The mat will protect us when we fall. And fall we will. There should be nothing quaint and proper about the rehearsal— delicate objects should be kept in the stage manager's office until the thrashing about is finished. Freedom has its price. We must be free when we rehearse: free to make mistakes, free to hit the walls, free to behave badly and apologize afterwards. The price is that we abandon the pretense of polite social conduct and meet each other bravely, squarely in the middle of the mat: to dance, to wrestle, to engage in the breathtaking act of creating something together, something new and alive. We should weather the occasional dents and bruises that come with learning to dance, or wrestle, because we trust each other, and if we do not, we should go home.

My God you are growing at such a rapid pace Andy. I never saw this coming. I was all set to have nice exchange of letters with you while I slipped into oblivion. But we make plans and God laughs, right? So let us embrace in robust collaboration Master Fallon. Set your compass and all sheets to the wind. I trust you. Will you trust me?

Love,
Alice

[printed script in blue ballpoint pen on stationery, "From the desk of Dr. Ian Pelli, 529 Windsor Ave, Narberth, PA" printed on each page]

6/27/05

Dear Alice,

Thanks for your letter. This is so weird. I actually had the phone in my hand and had to talk myself into putting it down so I could write to you. She wants letters she wants letters she wants letters. . . .

Did I scold you about your attitude? God I'm sorry if I did. My only point—and I stand by it—is that you are an example, both to the others at The Quad and to the Feasties. Whether you like it or not, we all look up to you. I hope it will come as no surprise to you that I have told the story of our letters to them and that I may have put you in an exalted light.

I understand you much better now. I see this project from your point of view and it makes sense that you're frightened. I see how I have stormed into your life and forced this R&J idea on you—it's all happening quickly isn't it? So I promise to be sensitive to what you, and others, have to work through as we create this thing, whatever it will become. I will honor and respect your authentic experience, as long as you honor the effect that experience has on others. When you roll your eyes at me and everyone sees it, it's a major ripple in our little pond.

Our "fight" (but I think that's too strong) made me think of this old actor I worked with in a new play about rodeo clowns at SoHo Rep in New York. His name was Earl and he was a Regional Theatre veteran, one of those actors who lives on the road six to eight months a year, doing plays in Cincinnati, Dallas, Seattle. Of the play we were rehearsing, he told me he took this job "which paid shit because he hadn't spent more than two months in his New York apartment in five years and he missed his dog." Anyway, I was fresh out of school and bouncing around like the pup I was, ~~causing a lot of~~ asking the director a ton of questions and fretting to anyone who'd listen about the answers I was or wasn't getting from him. Earl took me aside one night and gave me two pieces of advice:

"Son, here's what you do when the director tells you to do something. Look at the ceiling." I did. "Now look at the floor." I did. "Now look at the ceiling, now at the floor, that's it, keep repeatin' it." He was smiling, and I realized I was nodding, as in "yes." "Got that? Good. Then do whatever the hell you want, nine times out of ten they'll never notice. Here's the next thing. They can only say no when you ask for permission." And he slouched away.

It was my first taste of that actor/director schism you wrote about a couple of months ago. I was shocked. He seemed to advocate a kind of creative sabotage, and a complete breach of trust. But I took his advice and was generally lost throughout that production and a problem for the director, who was actually quite patient with me.

I resolved afterwards never to give a director an insincere nod of the head, to always ask questions. I resolved then (though I didn't have the words) to be a robust collaborator. It's the working it out that I <u>love</u>. His second point was more complicated though. I realized that I <u>had</u> been asking this poor director for permission to make choices, and what Earl was saying in his jaded way is that it's my professional responsibility to make choices without permission. But I would add it's also my responsibility to be flexible, accommodating, open-minded—and here's where you might be a bit rusty.

I love this idea we're developing, but I love you in the middle of it most. So you may call me director, but to me you are the Captain. Let our collaboration be robust and let the waters chop for all they're worth. A sailor needs a storm to take his measure.

See you soon,
Andy

[blue ballpoint pen on postcard, image of Philadelphia City Hall statue of William Penn on reverse]

7/1/05

Dear Alice—Do you know this guy? What's he got in his hand? Where have you been? Everything okay? I'm calling tonight! Love, Andy. [*The following in different handwriting:*] Hi Alice! Love, your Nurse Maya!

[printed script in blue ballpoint pen on stationery, "Mr. & Mrs. Howard Emlin" printed on each page]

7/3/05

Dear Alice,

Here's the list of the remaining workshops. I'd love for you to come to them all, but of course you should take care of yourself first: July 6, 7, 11, 13 and 14. We're continuing to work on scenes, observed by Barbara. She's also asked us to create a document for an acting class that we will share with each other. I thought I'd extend that invitation to you too. Let me know (by phone—you have my cell number—I know you do!) if you need a ride.

Everyone's worried about you. All they know is what you told me to tell them: that you fainted in the dining room and had to be taken to the hospital for observation. That's not far from the truth, is it?

As far as R&J is concerned, you let me know when you feel strong enough to have a look at what MF has come up with. It's basically a "greatest hits" from the play drawn from our readings and early rehearsals, with space in between for "non-fiction" scenes based on your life experience at The Quad. We are loosely following the Tectonic Theatre model—the ones who created The Laramie Project. We want to make art directly from life.

I'm staying with my grandparents for a while—it was getting a bit crowded at Maya's. I began to feel like I was really taking advantage of her parents, and I love my grandparents. ~~Maya can stay come~~ Mom's coming for an extended visit, you may meet her at one of the workshop sessions. Things are gathering on that front. I've been taking the train up to NYC once a week to meet with Dr. Kayne. It's been intense being back here, where I lived when I met you first, when Mom was facing the dark nights of her soul. How far ~~I've~~ we've come.

I'm so afraid of losing you, you have no idea. Please stay healthy. I wish you would tell me a little more about what's going on with you. Maya and I will be at Wallingford Meeting Sunday. See you there?

Love,
Andy

How to Rehearse a Scene for Class

I. Directly after the class in which the scene is assigned, exchange phone numbers and basic schedule information with your scene partner. Agree on a meeting time and place for a first read-through.

2. At the first read-through, read it once just sitting together, then have a discussion about it. What do you both think is going on in the scene? Where is the scene taking place? Begin to generate some ideas together about the answer to that question.

    Read the scene again, but this time go *very slowly*. Pull your chairs together so you can sit up and see each other. Try to lift your eyes off the page while the other is speaking, so you can begin to "hear" the lines coming at you. When you have a line, read ahead on the page and then try to lift your eyes off the page so you can speak to your partner. The point is to create as much eye-contact as possible. You will mess up, lose your place, giggle, feel embarrassed—this is all normal and *critically important to experience*. You and your partner are learning to trust each other, even when you both feel vulnerable, and you are beginning to speak in character.

    After this first rehearsal, begin to think about the other questions: Who is my character? What are they doing? How are they doing it?

3. Begin your next few rehearsals with the slow, eye-contact read-through described above. This will assist with memorization and you will be closing the gap between self and character. Then get up on your feet. Try things out using movement and

distance: walk around each other as you read-through, stand still, be close, be far away. Move around the "X Box":[36]

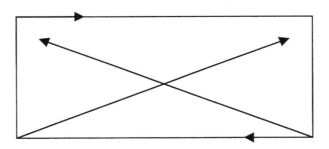

Shake things up: try shouting, try whispering. Slowly, the physical relationship that works best will become clear. When you feel ready, rehearse in a space where you can set up the rudimentary design you made up together for the scene. Do a read-through "on your feet" on this simple set. Make notes in your script about choices you like and repeat the ones you agree to keep.

4. By the beginning of the second week, each rehearsal should begin with a line-learning session. This replaces the "slow read-through." It's pretty simple: one of you holds the script and the other tries to do it "off-book." If you are "holding book" for a partner learning lines, here is my technique: never give a line unless asked for it (say "Line, please"). Sometimes hanging in the silence while looking for the line is important. Remember to breathe. Feed the asked-for line word by word.

---

[36]This is a simple floor pattern Andy developed to help beginning actors move while learning a scene.

Usually, the one learning lines will get it after a few words. *Then go back a few lines before the missed line, and start over.* This a critical step. Going back over the missed lines helps cement them. Be nit-picky. The actor's goal is to be word-perfect. If you are holding book and your partner substitutes an incorrect word, or drops a word, correct them. You may feel like a jerk, but your turn is next. Sometimes doing this on your feet on the set helps. We learn lines with our bodies as well as our minds, and sometimes that physical relationship you have with the other, or with the room, will become a part of the line. When you stand there in that agreed-upon spot, the line will come.

5. By the fourth or fifth rehearsal you should both be trying to do it off-book, on your feet and using a rudimentary set. Enlist a friend to be on-book for you and feed you lines when you drop them. As you begin to rehearse off-book, the world of your feelings will become more engaged. As your feelings become more engaged, you will forget your lines more and seem to take a step backwards. *You have not.* You are just getting used to multi-tasking: repeating memorized lines, reacting to your partner, feeling what you feel, moving someplace. This is the extraordinary work of the actor. It's hard—be gentle and forgiving with yourself. And yet, now is the time to take risks. Dare to provoke your partner, follow the impulse, imagine what your character would do in your ideal version of the scene, then do it.

6. After one or two rehearsals off-book, try scoring the scene for your character. Define what you are doing. *Write down your choices in your script* (this is why it's called "scoring," you are creating a score, as in a "musical score"). I will be checking your scoring when you bring the scene in to class. Challenge yourself: change that tactic from "intimidate him" to "squash him like a bug." Define a tactic you haven't quite fulfilled, but you're going for. *Always use a pencil, not a pen.* Scoring is a fluid process, and the score you create for your scene the first time you bring it in will probably not be the score you use the next time.

7. For the rehearsal before you show your scene in class (ideally the day before class), meet to make some final decisions, run through it once or twice and think of any questions you have for me or the class. I will question you on scoring and given circumstances when you bring the scene in, so double-check to make sure you have explored everything as fully as you can. *Remember: it's okay to show up and say, we're still thinking about that, or, I don't know yet.* I know the difference between a student who is searching and hasn't found the answer yet, and one who hasn't done the work.

It's also okay to disagree with your scene partner. This is difficult, but if you've come to an impasse about something, smile, shrug your shoulders, and bring the impasse in to class. Let us work it out for you. Try not to get hung up on being "right," which is impossible anyway.

The Basics:
- Aim for 3–4 hours of rehearsal per week. Be on time to your rehearsals. If you can't make one, call your partner in advance.
- Build trust through respect and humor.
- Have fun, be playful, yet disciplined.
- Don't get lost in your mind. Avoid yakking. Get up on your feet and move.
- Attend to the Four-Fold Way; avoid the Underlying Addictions.

[hand written in blue ballpoint pen, "Haverford College, Department of Fine & Performing Arts" embossed on the top of each page]

July 7th, 05

Dear Alice,

Our conversation has been continually on my mind since we had coffee last month. I've spoken to some colleagues about the whole Quaker identity issue here at Haverford and learned it's been a hot topic for some time. I was amazed to learn that the faculty was required to go to meeting for worship up through the fifties. You're right, the pendulum has swung to the opposite extreme, with some faculty regarding the presentation of spiritual ideas in higher education analogous to teaching a Harry Potter-type sorcery class. The good news is that it's an active discussion on this campus, with many folks deeply interested in the Quaker heritage of this school. I realized after speaking with you the other day that the big reason I'm afraid to present some ideas as "spiritual" in my class is that it means I have to examine my own relationship to those ideas, and be willing to share my own experience about them with my students. Yes, yes—I will look into what possibilities exist for a Quaker framework for this kind of creative exploration—I promise! But I may need some interpretive help from you . . .

I'm so glad to hear you're feeling better. We were all worried about you. We had a free-wheeling discussion in class last week about judgment, and it made me think about what you were saying about your time at the university. Andy went off about judgment being the "dark force" in education—it would have been comical if he hadn't been so serious. Martin played his antagonist, insisting that the teacher has to be able to label events in the classroom as good and bad, right and wrong. I offered one of your ideas, that we embrace the paradox: Andy and Martin are both right—it's the situation that changes.

I believe your experience with the tenure process was the apotheosis of the cult of judgment. When judgment is all teachers have then they wield it like a weapon, deriving satisfaction out of feeling right at someone else's expense. But I must ask you Alice—what role did you play in this drama thirty years ago? What mistakes did you make? It makes me sad to think of you teaching all those years, and no one watching you. It's an opportunity we so often miss in higher education, the opportunity to observe each other in the classroom and give each other advice in matters of pedagogy. This is why those conferences you avoided all those years are so important. It's where we get together and share our approaches. Perhaps it was your own fear which kept you away—fear that you might be changed by someone who has thought about it differently? It's the same fear that keeps us out of each other's classrooms: that if I watch someone who's really good, it will make me look really bad. All these thoughts were the genesis of the workshop you're now observing. I want to get acting teachers used to working together right at the start, so we can all become better at what we do, and avoid the isolation endemic in our profession.

Gathering in my mind are two things we touched on over coffee: the narcissistic actor and Stanislavsky. Susan and I rented a movie that made me think of our discussion about the way young actors create these intense fantasy worlds as they try to escape their real lives and carve out identities for themselves. The movie is called <u>Heavenly Creatures</u> and it's by Peter Jackson, the man who made the <u>Lord of the Rings Trilogy</u>. In it, these two girls have an intense relationship in which they engage in various fantasies which Jackson brings to life in the film. Neither of the girls are actors, but they're both feverishly creative. They invent alternative personalities for themselves, which resemble characters from a Romance novel, and they act out scenes together as these characters. What you begin to see though, is that the intensity of these fantasies is directly related to the agony of their adolescent lives. It's an over-the-top example of the link we were talking about between the cauldron of the adolescent psyche and the awakening obsession to escape through acting. What happens at the end of the movie takes this obsession to a gruesome extreme.

And re-reading <u>An Actor Prepares</u>, I found a startling example of a young actor escaping real-life pain through acting in the chapter called "Faith and a Sense of Truth." In section nine of that chapter, Kostya recounts watching a student named Dasha struggle with a scene from Ibsen's <u>Brand</u>. Dasha, Kostya tells us, had a child out of wedlock who died soon after birth. He says that Dasha continually sought out scenes with children in them. Some therapists call this "the will to repeat."

In the Ibsen scene, Dasha's character finds a child left on her doorstep, who later dies in her arms. Dasha performs it brilliantly and cries as she holds the "dead child," which is a log wrapped in a blanket. The students are deeply moved, and Kostya recounts that everyone wept. Tortsov praises her, but she wants to do it <u>again</u>. The poor girl is trying to bring her dead baby back to life. Tortsov allows her to do it again, but he has no knowledge of her real-life circumstances, and he asks her to relate to the log more like a real baby, as if she had lost a baby herself. She collapses in sobs, unable to continue. The students rush to her aid and comfort her, and Kostya tells Tortsov about Dasha's loss.

It's clear that a hundred years ago, Stanislavsky was aware of this phenomenon we were discussing: young people working out their pain through acting.
It's also clear that Stanislavsky regarded it as natural, certainly not a crime
against the art. He says that if Dasha comes across an analogous situation to her
own trauma in a play, it will be her "salvation." Not because she will regain
what was lost, but because she will be serving art by relating to her life-tragedy
creatively. He demonstrates the importance of the magic "if" in this section, too.
Dasha performs brilliantly when she relates to the scene in dramatic terms, as if
she were this <u>character</u>. The scene falls apart when she attempts to play the
scene as if the character was <u>her</u>, which occurs after Tortsov's inadvertent resur-
rection of her actual tragedy. I've always maintained that we get in trouble
when we play ourselves. We need to play characters. When Dasha empathizes
with the character she can play the scene releasing great emotion. But when she
confronts her own grief on its own terms, it overwhelms her.

One of the ways I stem the narcissism in my acting classes is I make my students work on plays—complete plays. I used to just hand out random scenes to
them, but now I choose two or three plays that will provide scene work for the
entire class and make everyone read all those plays. They bitch and moan about
it, especially when I tell them there will be a reading quiz on the assigned plays,
but the benefits have been confirmed to me after several years of doing this.
They are connected to a character's entire journey in a play, and we can talk
about what came before and what comes after the scene they're in. It involves
the other students in a much deeper discussion about the work they see, since
they formulate reactions to the plays, even the ones they're not in. Focus is
thrown on the characters' journeys and the class engages in a kind of group
research project on two or three plays. They sense early on that they are serving
a playwright's vision rather than their own narcissistic needs.

My kids come from a popular culture in which the distinction between fantasy and reality is becoming blurrier and blurrier. I know you don't watch a lot
of TV Alice, but there's been an explosion of these heinous things called "reality
shows." The camera is kind of voyeur, through which we get to watch non-
actors confronted with a variety of challenges, from the appalling, to the
boring, to the barely amusing. It's supposed to be more exciting because these
are "real people," but it's really an exercise in cultural narcissism. I worry that
my students begin to fantasize that they are seeing themselves in that little box.
These shows are a kind of fun-house mirror, which feed our obsession with sur-
faces. Creativity, intelligence and imagination are removed from the equation.

All we need to be on TV are a hot bod and a perky personality. There is no empathetic leap to take. It's enough to tune in and watch a bunch "real people" argue about who didn't do the dishes.

But as soon as you watch it on TV, it ceases to be real, and here's where the dangerous confusion begins. If it's happening on TV it must be okay and permissible, right? I laugh when people scratch their heads about why there's so much violence in the schools. Pop culture teaches kids that violence—physical, verbal, psychological—has no consequences. There was a show called <u>Jackass</u> in which these kids did all kinds of dangerous stuff for laughs, like throwing themselves out of windows. After a kid died imitating an episode from the show, they began putting a warning on before the show telling viewers not to try this at home. You'd think they'd have cancelled it.

And don't even get me started on video games. When Susan and I are out biking, we see these little kids outside on a beautiful day, focused with maniacal intensity on a hand-held plastic box that beeps and chirps, as they frantically push little buttons that make a kung-fu master beat up his assailants. Later as a teenager, on another beautiful day, these same kids will sit in front of their computers in a darkened room (so the screen is brightest), playing a soldier on a rampage in some virtual dungeon—killing and killing and killing. The world is violent enough. Just watch the news. Why must we reinforce it with our entertainment?

Standing in front of Andy and the others last week it dawned on me: this is why acting and theater and the teaching of it are so important. There is an epidemic of detachment in our young people. They are being anesthetized by media, which blurs the line between real experience and entertainment. Being an acting teacher is a clarion-call against this trend. Playing characters requires <u>empathy</u>, which is the opposite of the indifference and numbness many of my students arrive with. Our job is to wake up our young people: to their own feelings, to the events that happen right in front of them in the plays they study, to the possibility that they can understand these events and the fictional people they affect. Acting is a profound exercise in compassion, and the first person to find compassion for is the character you play. This is why I demand that my students speak of "him" or "her" instead of "me" when discussing character. This is how the narcissistic trend is reversed: empathizing with character leads to the healing of self, leads to a compassionate connection to the actual world. We should lift our students out of their lives, their bonds of self, and into the freedom of transformation. We must commit to the possibility of communion between human souls, as Stanislavsky describes it. Communion of this kind can only happen when we gather close to each other, in meetings, in classrooms, in theaters. We must pry our students away from their text messages and chat rooms and make them stand face to face, and not run away.

But what to do Alice, what to do about my students' pain, what to do about the spiritual aspect of acting, how do you speak of these things without invading personal space or coming across as religious zealot? We are distributing documents in the workshop now meant to help young actors in the classroom. I would love a contribution from you! Mine has to do with vocabulary. I'm experimenting with a concept I call "The Gift." It defines what the actor hopes to give the audience through his/her performance. Perhaps a way to steer focus away from self, and to engage the student actor in a spiritual act of generosity. We'll see.

Andy's doing great, by the way. I often fit my students into archetypes: the Rebel, the Company Man, the Queen, the Clown, etc. It's sort of a hobby. Andy is the Prophet—an unusual and rare archetype characterized by quiet intensity, an awkward relationship to group process and the ability to hush a room with his commentary. He carries a strange authority. He can be scary to teach, until you realize how vulnerable he is, and what an asset his insight can be.

Come to class soon!
Barbara

Questions and Vocabulary

The following are a series of questions you must explore for all scene work brought into class. In exploring these questions, we also define some important vocabulary, which we will use to talk about acting and the choices actors make. Remember there are no "right" and "wrong" answers. These questions are boundaries within which you and your scene partner's creativity is unleashed. I am not evaluating the "correctness" of your answers, but rather the depth of your creativity.

How does an actor make choices? What criteria does she use? I think an actor should ask three questions about any choice she makes:

- Does it serve the playwright? (Is it appropriate for this character and this scene? Does it enhance the playwright's vision?)
- Does it serve the audience? (Is it interesting, theatrical, provocative? Would I pay money to see someone do this in this scene?)
- Does it serve me? (Am I excited and/or challenged by this choice? Does it stretch me? Is it fun?)

Here are the basic questions that should be explored for all scene work brought in to class. They are listed in the usual sequence in which they are explored in rehearsal:

Who is my character?

The answer to this question describes the character you are playing. Obvious parameters are: age, appearance (you are required to approximate the clothes your character is wearing), occupation, personal history, physical issues (i.e., sickness, exhaustion, etc.). Included in this question is, who is my character in relation to the other(s) in the scene? Subtle, but important variations on this theme might be: what does my character dream of? what is my character's prayer? what is my character's secret? The answer to "who is my character" is mostly individual work each actor does on their character alone. *Your own imagination is the chief source of inspiration for this research.* You may catch yourself daydreaming about your character—seize these sleepy thoughts, they are often quite valuable. The ways in which your character is like or unlike you are important, too. But try to expand the investigation: who in your memory does this person remind you of? Where do you see this person today? As you go about your day, be on the look-out. Your character may walk right by you.

When we get to the final scenes, the play will offer an important source of information about your character. Pay attention to your character's behavior *throughout the play*, not just in the scene you are in.

Where is the scene?

This means creating a floor plan, or set design for your scene. Where are the doors and windows? What is beyond the lip of the stage (where the audience is sitting)? If your scene takes place in a building, what's the building like? What's the neighborhood like? What things (furniture, props, etc.) are in the scene, and which are most important? You are responsible for providing approximations of those things. *Mimed props are not permitted.* Also: where is the scene located geographically? What does it smell like? feel like? Odd personal associations are great, as long as you can describe them to us. This question should be explored collaboratively by both, or all, of the actors in the scene. Have a discussion and begin to make some choices together. Don't get too attached to ideas made early on. You may decide to move that sofa the day before you show the scene in class.

What is my character doing?

The answer to this question is called an **activity** or the **purpose**. The scene either begins with your character doing an activity or pursuing the purpose. It never begins with your character "doing nothing."

The **purpose** always has to do *specifically with another character*. It is a need your character has to get a result from someone else on stage, your objective. It describes something your character *wants the other to do, or admit or say*. Paradox: for the actor, it's best if your character *doesn't* get what she wants. So the best purposes for scene-work describe a need the character has that remains unfulfilled. If your purpose is never accomplished in the scene, it continues to pull you through it.

An **activity** describes what your character is doing when *what* your character is doing isn't connected to anyone else on stage. The best activities are physical. Your character might be "cleaning up," or "getting ready to go out," or "making a meal." If you decide your character begins your scene with an activity rather than a purpose, you must look for the moment when the purpose begins. The activity may continue, but with the beginning of the purpose, the actor's attention has focused on the other character. Important: most scenes begin right away with a purpose for each character.

Sometimes, a character's purpose changes during the course of a scene. A change of purpose usually occurs when a new character enters, somebody exits, or a "bomb" explodes during the scene: a secret is revealed, an accusation is made, a betrayal occurs, a love is announced, or any physical act of love or violence (a kiss or a slap). A purpose change is delineated by a horizontal line through the script, as is the beginning of a purpose.

How is my character doing it?

This is called the **tactic:** it is how your character executes his purpose. There are two general kinds of tactics: tactics that *pull or seduce*, and tactics *that push or threaten*. Your job is to define the different tactics your character uses in sequence to execute his purpose. A useful starting point for scoring tactics is to ask, Is my character "pulling closer" or "pushing away" the other character here? Once you've decided if your character is pushing or pulling the other person, the tactic can be described as a verb: *humor her*, or *intimidate him*.

The goal of the tactic is to achieve your purpose. Example: If my character's purpose is "to get her to admit she's wrong," my tactic choices might be:

cajole her (pulling)
intimidate her (pushing)
sympathize with her (pulling)

These are three ways to get her to admit she's wrong, which is my purpose. If I have chosen wisely, she will never admit she's wrong in the scene and so I am constantly engaged.

Often, your character will meet **obstacles** while pursuing his purpose. An obstacle might be his own fear, or an interruption of some kind. Most often, it's the other character. Your partner's purpose, tactics and behavior may be obstacles your character must overcome to achieve his/her purpose. Obstacles can make your character change tactics, as your character tries different ways to achieve his purpose and maneuver around the obstacles he encounters. If your character has more than one tactic, you will end up dividing your scene in to several "bits" delineated by a sequence of tactics. Tactic changes are marked with the sideways "T" when they occur quickly.

Occasionally, a **transition** takes place between tactics, or in the rare case that your character changes purposes. Any transition (between purposes or tactics) has four steps. These fours steps may take place over the course of a few pages, or they may take place almost instantaneously. The four steps in a transition are:

1. Something new attracts your character's attention.
2. Your character examines the new object of attention more and more closely.
3. A catalyst ignites inside your character.
4. A new purpose is pursued or a new tactic is initiated.

It's important not to rush transitions, and investigating these fours steps during a transition will help with specificity.

The Gift

Remember that acting is a service you provide an audience. If you are a professional, they pay money to receive something from you. But I like to think of what I give my audience less as a "product" and more as a "gift." I have acted for free many times, and I believe that a person's creativity is God-given and never for sale. It is given in the spirit it is made: freely.

So the last question to ask yourself is this: What is the **gift** I am giving my audience with this scene? Is it the opportunity to understand themselves better? If so, how? Is it the chance to laugh and let go of their problems? If so, laugh at/about what? Be as specific as you can. Write your gift, or notes about it, at the beginning of your scene. And don't worry about not being able to "nail this one down." Always continue exploring. Don't worry about getting the answers "right." Live in the questions.

Writing down your character's purpose, tactic choices and gift in your script constitutes the "score" for your character. Remember: actors make discoveries **while rehearsing on their feet**. An actor's score isn't a series of intellectual decisions made in advance based on ideas that occur while reading. There are no "right" or "wrong" choices, though there may be choices which help you and choices which hinder you. That's where I come in: I assist you in making compelling choices. The only way to fail is to make no choice at all.

Play first. Score last.

[Alice's workshop observation, blue ballpoint pen on white, lined notebook pages]

July 10th, 2005

Brilliant point about <u>using</u> what you distribute in class, about creating demonstrations. Barbara has come into her own. Yes, her vocabulary will [*illegible*] and confuse a beginner—you must <u>show</u> them a Purpose performed, or a Tactic played. This is when you seize and freeze. Or just as she did with Joslyn as Roberta, saying "Pursue the Purpose more!" or "Play the Tactic more strongly!" Then these ideas leap from the page and are activated.

I also like her criteria for making choices, and when to score. For God's sake, don't get [*illegible*] by this business of which words to use. It's simple: the character wants something and tries to get it in different ways. Students must understand that this business of scoring, of using words like Purpose or Objective or Task or Intention or Action or Tactic—whatever vocabulary you teach, and one's as good as another—they must understand that these words represent discoveries made <u>while playing</u>, and are not intellectual ideas imposed while reading. She writes, Play First, Score Last—yes! I think she gets too complicated with the rest of it, though. It should have been one page, not four.

We must strive for simple language in acting classes, and maybe this is my Quaker sensibility speaking, but acting is slippery and complicated and contradictory enough without mucking up its investigation with [*unclear: jargon?*] Choose the vocabulary you will teach and then simplify it to its essence. This is a lifelong winnowing. Teach them what the terms mean by linking them to events the students witness or experience. Be consistent. In my opinion, the essence is this: it's a two-way street all the time, the actor effects, and is affected by, the other.

And be playful. Jargon has a deadening effect. Make the <u>thing created</u> most important, and damn the terminology from time to time. The proof is in the pudding isn't it? An actor may bring in a brilliant scene, and he hasn't failed if he's still confused about what a Tactic is. He's just instinctual. Nudge the instinct from his dreaming place into his frontal lobe. As long as students know that these terms are only meant to help define their own creativity, their own choices, you're okay. When students start burying themselves in handouts like these, looking for the "answers," then you have a small textbook problem on

---

your hands. Take the ideas, put them on their feet and run them around. The actor must stay connected to that dreaming place, which is where the deep creativity comes from. You are just giving him names for the energy formed there.

Oh dear, here goes Martin again. You know, the narcissism of Alice Miller's investigation can infect the acting teacher too. It's an enticing trap. Here you have these [unclear: vessels? vassals?]—your students—who know nothing about acting and will cling to every word you say as holy writ. Most of them are desperate to succeed, and if they are young they are likely grappling with the issues of identity and transference I described in my early letters to you. They are in a heightened state of desire and vulnerability. Along comes a wounded teacher, whose only source of self-esteem is the adulation he gets in class and the control he wields there, and so he wields it autocratically. Then a nightmare of reciprocal neuroses begins: the teacher feeding his narcissism by creating a closed system dominated by his "insights" only, and the students who cling to him in the belief that he will give them the keys to success, or an end to their pain, and in their desire to "get it right" affirm his closed system, convincing Teacher of his supremacy (the worst directors behave this way too). That man who shouted at me in the <u>Glass Menagerie</u> scene was such a teacher. The pity is they're so common, such is the demand for acting classes. It's why Barbara's workshop is such a great idea, because Martin has again been (gently) reprimanded for talking too much and dominating the discussion. Does this mean he will become a great teacher? Who knows. But it's a darn sight better than groping along in the dark, which is how I learned to teach.

Now you've handed out your contribution, "How to Rehearse a Scene." Well, done, Andy. It never occurred to me—we send these kids away to rehearse a scene and they haven't got a the foggiest notion of what that means. I like the way you incorporate the Four-Fold Way into it, and the way you speak to the experience of the beginning actor—the [unclear: embarrassment?]. Your compassion for the beginner is exemplary.

I just offered my handout. Looks of mild shock from the participants when the crazy old woman who scribbles in her wheelchair participates!

Alice's Recipe for an Acting Class

1. **Understand the context.** What are your institution's expectations? Who are your students? How do your goals mesh with the first two questions?

2. **Be organized.** Actors need structure to be safe. Practice good time management, have lesson plans to guide you, be clear about deadlines, expectations and the shape of the semester.

3. **Be a role model.** Have fun, demonstrate your love for theater, share your professional experience, be disciplined, express your feelings without shame, provoke achievement through inspiration.

4. **Mind the three Cs:**
   - Consistency. Create a common vocabulary and stick with it, apply criticism evenly, enforce expectations.
   - Compassion. Remember how hard it was for you, focus on what the student is doing that works, counteract fear with humor.
   - Coherence. Speak simply and identify specific moments to illustrate larger concepts, chart each student's progress, make sure your assignments are understood.

5. **Serve the ensemble.** Every student is paying to be there. Group experience can happen in each class.

6. **The 15% Solution.** Scenes no longer than 15% of total class time. When in doubt, shorter is better.

7. **Teach respect.** For the classroom, for each other, but most of all, for the art itself.

8. **Live in the questions.** Invite feedback, admit ignorance, seek the Spirit, name the paradoxes, love the process.

9. **Connect to the world.** Apply the principles away from class, put the actor in a larger context.

10. **Train the Total Actor.** Balancing mystery with practicality, we stimulate body, mind, and spirit.

[blue fountain pen on hand-made, heavyweight stationery]

July 15th, 2005

Dear Alice,

Firstly, it's been so great to get to know you. And to act with you. I confess when our eyes meet sometimes it makes me nervous. It feels like you're looking into my soul! It's weird enough playing your Nurse! This explains the "hiccup" you noted, when you said to me "Play the thought on the line! Don't pause!" You see, it's your fault I take those little pauses—I'm not used to being looked at like that! (at least not on stage . . .) I promise to get better. Watch out! Next time I'm going to look into <u>your</u> soul!

Alice, I need your advice. I've been offered a job working with a theater company in Philly. Andy doesn't know, and I can't talk to my parents about it because I know what they'll say—they're crazy to have me close by. But the idea of doing the long distance relationship thing with Andy—I can't bear it. Moveable Feast is great, but after the Philly Fringe we're supposed to go on tour to other Fringes. Being on the road like that is really hard for me and we're all so poor. This offer is with a company and it's ideal. They do the kind of European physical work I love. It's not a lot more money, but if I lived at home I wouldn't have to temp. I'd just work with them (developing new work, performing, and running their education outreach program).

I really want to do this, ~~but I don't want to leave~~—God this is embarrassing to write about! No wonder people don't write letters anymore! You have to see what you're thinking!—I don't want to choose between Andy and this job. There—I ~~said~~ wrote it.

Alice, will you be my secret weapon? Will you drop the idea into his head that he could live and work down here? He's so ambitious—he's actually a little obsessed. New York is good for some people—they thrive there. I don't think Andy's one of those people. The city plays to all his worst tendencies—competition, insecurity, compulsiveness. He told me once that it crushes him, being on the subway, and realizing that everyone on it with him has dreams with the same meaning to them that his have to him.

With all the work he's doing on teaching, at that workshop and so forth, I know he could find a teaching position here, maybe at one of the local theaters teaching adult classes just to start. Maybe my Dad could help him out at UArts. And I know he's a good actor. Plus he's cute, which never hurts. Please don't say anything to Andy about all this—not yet.

You seem so wise to me. I thought of speaking to you about it during a break from R&J rehearsal, but Andy's there, and anyway I thought if I wrote it down I could think about it more clearly. And I wanted to break into the letter writing thing you and Andy have going, I felt left out! I tried to <u>not</u> write this letter, but when I thought about who to talk to about it all, I just kept coming back to you. You've become my Old Auntie I never had!

Peace,
Maya

[script in black fountain pen on embossed stationery, "The Quad, Swarthmore, Pennsylvania" printed on the top of each page]

Dear Andy,

I had to take home my notes from the workshop and organize them. I'm afraid my frantic scribbling while I watch is becoming more and more illegible—even to me. An effect, I'm afraid, of my downward spiral. Here in my apartment I can take my time to write clearly, and what I saw today was too important to be lost in old woman's scrawl. I have to say it again: you are developing by leaps and bounds. You can't see it, because you're inside yourself. But free from the demons that were holding you back, your Inner Light has come ablaze and it is astonishing to witness.

It was an extraordinary class. You peeled open the can of worms called "crying" today. This is that scene from that play about the <u>Deep Blue Sea</u> by John Shanley. A bit vulgar, but still it seems more appropriate for your generation than some of the old chestnuts Barbara is so fond of. But her strategy of having you work on scenes as teachers in front of each other is a stroke of genius. You were working with Joslyn and Larry, and you were magnificent.

Before the scene began Joslyn was agitated and the classroom was tense. You had all seen the scene before and you all knew how high-stakes it was. You joked with the class softly. I felt the tension begin to ease. You lightly teased Joslyn about her nervousness.

"Hey! You're bouncing off the walls!" She laughed at herself. "Look, you're supposed to be nervous," you said, "if you aren't, there's something wrong with you. But you don't need to fan the flames. It's your creative juices, is all. How will you focus them?"

The scene began and Joslyn was squeezing emotion, over-focusing on Larry/Danny, reaching for a feeling. She employed all the tricks a self-involved actor will when she feels she should be crying: keeping her eyes open to induce watering, contorting her face, hyper-ventilating. There's almost nothing worse than an actor obsessed with his or her own feelings. And yet it is a phase we must pass through, and we teachers need to know how to assist this passage without shaming the actor.

"Let's start again," you said. "Look, the feelings aren't in the words. What's Roberta doing?" Then there was a discussion about given circumstances. Joslyn confessed she didn't know what Roberta wanted in the scene, and in a moment of insight, you activated that problem. You decided that she'd lost something, she didn't know what it was, but she thought it was in the room with Danny. Searching for what is lost became her activity. Then you derailed the over-focusing: "You don't need to look at Larry so much" you told her. "I can see you two are connecting well."

The scene began again. They were both more active and less self-conscious—Joselyn/Roberta moving around the room, Larry/Danny following like a wounded dog. "You can't forgive me!" Roberta cries, and Joslyn teetered on the edge of a big feeling. You moved to a position about five feet in front of them and spoke very quietly, while they continued in the scene.

"Sit on the bed" you told her. She did. Danny sat next to her. "See him now," you said. She did. Danny said, "You're forgiven." They continued. "He loves you," you said. The tears came. "Breathe. Don't let it run away from you" you told her, and you moved back to your seat. Danny takes her crying over his knees and gently spanks her, the scene played through to its conclusion—a wonderful performance, active, moving, devoid of sentimentality. During the commentary on the scene afterwards, you didn't refer to her tears once.

Here's what you did right: first, you adjusted the atmosphere in the room. Often, the nervous student is [unclear: ashamed?] of being nervous, or wishes to deny it in an attempt to appear "confident," and in so doing (paradoxically) increases her own nervousness. You wiped this syndrome out by calling Joslyn on it gently and humorously, allowing her to laugh and to release some excess feeling and begin to focus on the task at hand.

Your second accomplishment was your first intervention. It was the second time in for the scene. Working through first is appropriate the second time in. You could see right away that the scene wasn't going to progress because of the partners' over-focus on each other, Joslyn's self-involvement and a general lack of action. An actor squeezing emotion usually becomes divorced from a creative relationship to her own body, and either becomes frozen (as Joslyn was) or stomps about and throws things in an attempt to jump-start some magnifi-cent feeling (more common with men—we saw you do it as Eddie recently). You got her re-connected with the basics: what does Roberta want, how is she going to get it and what is she physically doing in the scene? Joslyn couldn't articulate what Roberta wants (her purpose), and rather than forcing an answer on her, you left it blank but suggested she was "looking for some-thing," an idea Joslyn seized on which activated her. Thus the actor's journey and the <u>character's</u> journey were synchronized, a phenomenon that leads to a powerful, truthful performance.

Paradoxically, you created character/actor separation, by exploring with Joslyn <u>Roberta's</u> given circumstances, and in so doing [unclear: stimulated?] Joslyn's sense of empathy for Roberta, which began to replace Joslyn's obsession with self. It is this empathy for character, for the <u>other</u>, which is the key to genuine feeling for the actor. This is where Strasberg got it so wrong, focused as he was on the <u>actor's</u> process of generating emotion.

Your third accomplishment was your second intervention. Sensing that Joslyn was on the verge of crying and was ready to cross that threshold; knowing that that release of feeling is appropriate for Roberta and honors Shanley's play; believing that an acting class is where we learn to creatively work with our feelings, you fed in some simple side-coaching to Joslyn as she played: "See him," "He loves you," "Breathe, don't let it run away with you." These side-coachings were delivered from a kneeling position in front of Joslyn (this was the only time I saw any of the student teachers get up out of the chair). You kept enough distance between you and the actors to preserve their sense of intimacy—you didn't break in, as it were, and your words were delivered quietly and directly. Joslyn knew you were there and knew exactly what you were up to—she said so afterwards. No one was trying to [unclear: manipulate?] anyone else. You nudged her through a doorway and she obliged—<u>her choice</u>.

With the exception of "He loves you," your coaching had to do with physical adjustments and had nothing to do with Joslyn's or Roberta's inner state. "See him" suggested that perhaps she had found what she was looking for. "He loves you" gave voice to the piece of information that Roberta resists the most: that she is worthy of love in spite of her terrible transgression. Notice that you didn't say "You love him." Your coaching encouraged Joslyn to take in her scene partner (who had ceased manufacturing intensity, and was simply, beautifully, there for her.) You didn't command her to adopt <u>your</u> perception of her character's emotional landscape. You encouraged her to share herself more fully with him and therefore with us. It was a note more about Danny than Roberta. "Breathe, don't let it run away with you," said as the sobs overwhelmed her—as a big feeling frequently will the student actor—you guided her back to the <u>work</u>, lifted her off the feeling and put Joslyn, not the feeling, in charge.

Lastly, there was no praise of the crying during the commentary—either by you, Miss Lewis or the students, who were visibly moved. You cried, too, Andy, and you joked about it when the scene broke: "Got me . . ." you said, with a wry smile on your face. Then you moved on. The scene work was discussed and applauded, the crying itself wasn't. The conversation revolved around how much more focused the scene became in response to your first intervention, and how powerful it was to watch them play the scene in spite of the feelings. What moves us is not actors crying, but Roberta and Danny moving forward in the face of their grief and confusion. We should bring no special reverence to feelings expressed, and this is an important lesson: expressing feelings is part of the work, not the work itself. Feelings deserve no more and no less attention than any other aspect of the actor's work, from line-learning to physical choices. And yet the paradox: great teachers are the ones who aren't ashamed to let their feelings show.

How do we square this emotional work with the fact that so many young people study acting with narcissistic motives, motives that involve expressing feelings impermissible in their own lives, motives based in real pain and a real need to break from that pain and forge a true identity? One way, I'm sure, is to de-emphasize the expression of feelings in actor training, and to reinforce the empathetic work of playing characters. Barbara thinks we've got to get away from talking about what "you" are feeling when you act, and ask instead what "he"—the character— is doing. We need to move away from the first and second person, and into the third. Stanislavsky is clear: feelings cannot be manufactured, it's a waste of time, if they come, let them come. And if they don't come but the director is [unclear: demanding?] them, well, then there's your bag of tricks.

A friend of mine had to do an exercise for Sandy Meisner called "Enter Crying." It is exactly what the title suggests. Actors whipped themselves into tears in the hallway outside his classroom in order to enter the scene crying. My friend snorted water from the hallway bubbler up his nose and [unclear: garnered or gained] praise from the great Master for the tears streaming down his cheeks as he entered. Another friend who's on TV a lot now can make herself cry the way other people can wiggle their ears. It's a party trick. I'm sure that this talent used judiciously on stage could move me. I'm reminded of that Mamet book you recommended, where he writes that acting is the art of illusion, an illusion to serve an audience. I don't care how that illusion is generated. If it is generated with great skill and used appropriately, chances are it will be effective.

But I have also witnessed plenty of crying actors who have left me cold. So I don't think it's the event of producing tears that moves the human heart. I believe it gets back to Stanislavsky's Rays. I believe that the human being in the throes of _real_ feeling charges the atmosphere with spiritual energy that is received by other human beings. I believe it because I _feel_ it—this is the Quaker part. Our Quaker experience is feeling-based, as opposed to intellectually reasoned. Josylyn/Roberta and Larry/Danny experienced a release of grief, grief for Danny and Roberta, and _indirectly_ for themselves. That release generated Rays of feeling which shot across the room and were felt by everyone there. These are the same Rays communicated by great Spiritual ministry. I believe what separates us from animals is our exquisite capacity for empathetic feeling, and I believe that this capacity is Divine in nature. When I am moved by someone else, the hair on my neck rises, a stone drops in my gut, or my face burns, or my eyebrows arch, or I smile, or my eyes fill with tears, or I [unclear: burst or bust] out laughing. These are spiritual events born on the wings of feeling. Through another person, God is moving me.

There are great actors who can come on stage and seem to do absolutely nothing, and yet fill a giant theater with dread—or bring it to gales of laughter. The context of those appearances matter, but they have the effect they do through spiritual transmission, I'm convinced. Sure, you can trick me, and that's fine. We will always be part showman. But a good actor, possessed of his bag of tricks, nevertheless uses it sparingly. He seeks to be more minister than showman, and a minister serves others through spiritual revelation, sent and received as feelings. This gets back to the Bates book. Actors are shamans, undergoing transformation for spiritual effect.

These transformations create new life, new life witnessed only once in the moment of performance, and only by those in attendance. We give birth to characters, and today you were the midwife. The best midwives have given birth themselves, so please keep acting Andy, and bring what you learn back to your students.

Thanks for having me in this workshop. I realized watching all of you that I have so much to say, and you've given me a chance to say it. Perhaps that's what's made me grumpy these past several years, the sense that I had something to say and no audience. You have been my audience and I'm forever grateful. Grateful, too, to your fellow student teachers. I'm afraid I was a distraction there, and I confess I felt out of place. You all are so young, so vital. I feel like an old [unclear: dinosaur?]. I realize that as much as I'd like to believe that I should have been Teacher Barbara, I never could have mustered the energy she had to help you become better teachers. It's like your friend from the

Feast company said: "Mortality sucks." I must stop coming to class now. It makes me too tired and the doctor has warned me about "overdoing it."

Speaking of Moveable Feast, I can't conceive of doing our <u>Romeo Geriatric</u> as anything other than some kind of dog and pony, one-night-stand at the Quad. I know you have grand aspirations for it, but I'm not well enough to walk to lunch downstairs six times a week, much less play Juliet, even in the truncated version you've all created. Sometimes I think we've all simultaneously gone completely batty doing this "age reversed" thing you're so hot about. And sometimes I think it's only my vanity that keeps me involved. But I do like that Maya. And it's a damn sight better than watching television.

So I'll see you and the rest of the aborigines tomorrow night for more mucking about with Shakespeare and the aged. Don't misunderstand the [*unclear: weariness or wariness*] of a tired, old woman. You have been an unexpected bright light in my dusk.

Love,
Alice

[script in black fountain pen on embossed stationery, "The Quad, Swarthmore, Pennsylvania" printed on the top of each page]

July 17th, 2005

Dear Barbara,

I must take my leave of you and your fine workshop. It was quite a class we had this afternoon, but I am not doing so well and I need to preserve what little strength I have left.

Good luck with your tenure application. What mistakes did I make? Plenty. Firstly, I never understood, nor took the time to find out what this university wanted of me. Never mind the fact that this information wasn't offered, I should have ferreted it out. I taught my classes the way I wanted to teach them, believing naïvely that this was just fine with everyone. I suspect it was not. My other mistakes were interpersonal. On a couple of occasions early on, I lost my temper with my colleagues. One would think the rash behavior of a new faculty member to be forgivable. In my case it was not. I acted out in some ways that I was barely aware of, those behaviors being the result of the "familial paradigm" manifesting in unfortunate ways. The wounded daughter fought back, and my esteemed colleagues were frightened. But as I say, this was who I was. There was little I could have done about it, even if I had been aware of what was going on with me and had desired to change. From what I've learned of your department and your circumstances, it sounds hopeful. I am gratified that you will continue practicing the art you teach, and that your institution and your colleagues support you in your art.

I enjoyed your archetypes—I'd never thought of it that way. Andy as a prophet. What you call his "authority" I might call "authenticity." How paradoxical that one, as wounded as he, found his authenticity playing other people.

Please stay in touch. Andy has me involved in this absurd production of Romeo and Juliet. How absurd? I'm playing Juliet. Anyway, I'm sure he'll let you know if we ever choose to share it with an audience, a prospect I am [unclear: dubious?] about.

I do hope there is more coffee and tea in our future. Give my best to Susan.

Alice

PS: The best books I have ever read on teaching are Parker Palmer's <u>The Courage to Teach</u> and Mary Rose O'Reilley's <u>Radical Presence</u>. They may speak to your condition in this coming year.

[printed script in black felt-tip pen on stationery, "Mr. & Mrs. Howard Emlin" printed on each page]

7/21/05

Dear Alice,

Thank you for yet another extraordinary letter. I had a hard time reading it, which was good, because it made me slow down and concentrate. I had little memory of what I did that day with the Danny scene—I was in "instinctual reaction mode" or something. ~~You help me understand things so much~~

Crying was always this badge of honor when I was studying acting in high school and college: "Whoa! He cried! Intense!" It meant your were ~~brill~~ a Truly Great Actor, and so a lot of us tried desperately to cry in our scenes. It was usually really embarrassing. The worst part of it looking back is that any of us thought for a moment that we would fool anyone with our artificial gasps for breath, tightened larynxes and dry eyeballs. My public humiliation was as Treplev in the infamous "head bandaging" scene from The Seagull.[37] My teacher mocked me to the class, doing an imitation of my contorted face while trying to cry. He ~~kicked my~~ opened an acting class can of whup-ass on me. But then each semester, there were always one or two scenes in which someone sent the Rays flying, and we who received them would wipe the tears from our eyes and think "Damn, I wish I could do that."

It is the witnessing of the actor that sparks Stanislavsky's Rays. While I was working with Joslyn and Larry, I became aware of being watched and the sensation that my back (I was facing away from the class) was getting warm. I'm convinced that Joslyn and Larry felt profoundly aware of being witnessed, and that that connection to the audience fed the emotional release. This is why I've always rejected the notion of the "fourth wall," which closes off the actor from the audience. The actor needs to feel the audience with her, and then give them something. An actor giving herself something shuts out the audience. ~~It's like sex~~

The supportive, ensemble nature of the class is important, but great performances are fueled by risk and the vulnerability generated by performing for

---

[37]This an explosive scene between the great actress Arcadina and her son Constantin (Treplev) in the middle of act III.

THE ACTOR'S WAY

people unknown to you, and the knowledge that if you ~~fuck~~ mess up, you can't start over. Sometimes I wonder if we are teaching our students to rehearse, rather than to perform. They are two very different experiences. I wonder if there's a place for an acting class that has an invited audience once a month.

Of course I'm disappointed that you don't want to share Romeo Geriatric with a wider audience. I'm so proud and excited by the work we've done together. More than anything, I love the intermingling of young and old—the way you and Maya disappear during breaks to gossip, the dirty jokes shared by Ed and Sam, the "robust collaboration" between me and Ernie—the stubborn S.O.B! If nothing else, we have made our own little community. It's been very satisfying. You told me a couple of days ago that it's been good for "your mood." So stop pretending you're not enjoying it! We have a fine little 75 minute piece, so let's share it with The Quad, with the Wallingford Friends' Meeting Arts Festival and for one night at The Playground downtown. Agreed? We'll forget about a run in the fall somewhere. Age-reversed theater! It's the wave of the future!

Mom went back to Massachusetts last weekend. It was great to have her here these last couple of weeks, all shacked up with her folks—Grandma and Grandpa Emlin. I told her about the booze, or the not-booze as it stands now. At first she thought it was all her fault. I had to calm her down about that. When we moved to Newton in '92 I went to a big public high school (sort of the anti-WFS). I fell into the artsy crowd there, which was a lot like the artsy crowd at WFS, except we smoked pot. And drank. But so did everyone else. Mom said she knew and wished she had done more to intervene. I said it wouldn't have made a difference. At that point the damage was done.

You know that sinking ship we were discussing last spring? Well I'm back on board and the damn thing won't sink. In fact it's floating again and the view from the bridge is fine. Those are some excellent ripples you've been sending my way, Teacher Alice.

My sublettor called. He wants to know if I'm coming back in September, cause he loves the place and wouldn't mind staying on. We begin working on Dust again in a few weeks, moving from the UArts residency to actually rigging the space where we'll be performing it downtown at the Fringe in September. So I could stay through August and then commute down here for the shows in September. But—and I can't believe I'm writing this—I'm thinking of telling him to take the place for another year.

Maybe it's because I'm riding a Pink Cloud,[38] but I love the way I've felt around here the last couple of months. I keep meeting all these cool people who live and work here. Some of them even have families of their own. And Maya's been offered a job down here. A really cool job with a physical theater company called Pig Iron. I'm jealous. When I think of returning to NYC all I feel is . . . dread. But then I feel dread at the thought of <u>not</u> returning. Christ, I've spent the last seven years there trying to make IT happen for myself. I'm freelancing with two agents, I work semi-regularly, TAG wants me back, Moveable Feast wants to take <u>Dust</u> on the road. I have a nice little apartment I can barely afford. ~~Things are~~ I'd be insane to throw that all away, for what? To work down here in the provinces? Philadelphia? It's the bastard child of east-coast cities, stuck in between New York and D.C., stinking in its insecurity. Haven't I admitted defeat if I leave New York? Doesn't that make me a loser?

Maya and I are going to Hershey Park this weekend. Wanna come?

Love,
Andy

&

---

[38] "Pink Cloud" is an AA term for a common euphoria experienced in early recovery. It is a temporary condition.

THE ACTOR'S WAY

[script in black fountain pen on embossed stationery, "The Quad, Swarthmore, Pennsylvania" printed on the top of each page]

July 27th, 2005

Dear Andy,

Have you ever heard of the astrological phenomenon known as "Saturn Returns?" I first heard the term in 1966. A fellow student I was sweet on at U Mass was an amateur astrologer—the worst kind, inclined to forecast epic events from scant study. But to me then, he and his star-charts were exotic and compelling. I was struggling with my Angel, thinking (again) of running away to New York, feeling like I had cheated myself of a life of glamour and excitement for one of responsibility and plainness. I was distraught. Charles told me that I was in the midst of a profound astral [unclear: re-alignment?], when the foundation of one's adult life is created; and if that foundation is sound, good things may be built on it, and if it is flawed, the cracks will be exposed. He said it described the return of the planet Saturn to the place it held in the heavens when one was born. This happens for most people between 28 and 32 years of age. He said it is a time of profound psychological transition.

If you think about it, that period in one's life is a time of profound psychological transition with or without the ringed planet having some influence. Who doesn't squirm a bit around one's 30th birthday? But your last letter brought Charles back to my mind, and I thought, Andy's Saturn is returning.

As artists, we not only live our lives, we [unclear: interpret?] them. Our lives are epic to us, they should be, they provide us with the bright or murky colors to paint with. Our lives make our music, move us across stages and bring our characters to life. The only value astrology has ever had for me is in the poetic interpretation it offers of what's happening in my life. So step back, Master Fallon, and ask yourself: what's happening in your life? How are your constellations lining up? And what message can you divine from the patterns you witness?

Your ministry in Meeting last Sunday (delivered haltingly, vulnerably, beautifully) was about what the Divine feels like in your life. You said that for you, the most compelling notion offered by the Religious Society of Friends is the Quaker position that Divinity can be experienced, viscerally, every day. So feel it now, Andy. The Inner Teacher is speaking. Lucky you, dear boy, it seems s/he is speaking quite clearly. Now you need to answer.

I will not tell you to leave New York and move to Philadelphia, as much as I like having you around to whisk me away to amusement parks. God knows I love both cities. But you have been transient your whole life, and now Saturn returns and wants to know where to lay the foundation. The fog is lifting from your soggy brain, you have love in your life (and she's quite a catch—if you let her slip away you're a rank fool) and you have tasted the sweet, old [unclear: aroma or ambrosia] of community. Best of all, the ghost isn't haunting you here.

Oh, you know, the ghost of Fame. It's the one that chases you to an audition you don't want to go to, because it could be your lucky break. It's the one that makes you bow and scrape before people you don't respect because the ghost is hungry, and they have the food. It's the one that keeps you awake at night wondering what you need to do, to be, to transform into in order to grace the cover of a magazine. It's the ghost that reminds you of what you're not—pretty enough, tall enough, good enough, sexy enough. This is the one that sits next to you at the movies and points to the screen, whispering, "That should be you." Every now and then, driven by the phantom lash, one in one thousand of us gets that Film/TV/ Broadway role. But the haunting doesn't end there, the ghost simply asks, "Now what?" Most who are [unclear: afflicted or affected] with this ghost end up like my old friend with the fixed smile; writing invitations in the darkness to people he doesn't know, so that he might be propelled to a life he only ever dreamed of, slowly becoming a ghost himself.

Philadelphia's great virtue and great curse, if you're an actor, is that you can't get famous here. There's a ceiling—you can only go up so far. The same is true, more or less, of every other city in the United States except Los Angeles. The Hungry Ghosts can't haunt us in these cities because there's no [unclear: taunt or tease] of fame. There's only the work. For many in New York, you do a play so that you will get to do that other play/TV show/film. I remember thinking of some of my fellow actors there that they weren't really there, on stage, rehearsing with me. They were obsessing about the unknown next thing, which was always more important. Nothing artistic in Philadelphia is that much more important than anything else (though some will try to puff themselves up). It's all theater or dance, song or paintings, offered up for it's own virtues. It is all equally, exquisitely important, just because it is art.

So in an effort to employ some Quaker spiritual guidance, let me pose you some queries:[39]

Why be an actor if fame is removed from the equation?

Where do you want to make your home?

What else is important to you besides acting, and will acting tolerate being second or third in your life to other priorities?

Yes, people make art and have families here—a revolutionary development. I was raised in an age in which we were taught that those two things were mutually exclusive. One needed to throw oneself prostrate at the alter of his art. But that was my Angel to wrestle with. And I now see that the teachers who told me I had to make a choice between having an acting career and having a home were forcing their own bitter sacrifice on to me. It's the old saw: you have to do it the way I did it because I did it that way. The prophets, the ones who rebelled, who tried to have families and artistic careers were told, you're being grandiose, you think you can have it all; or, all you'll ever make is watered-down art, because your devotion is not [unclear: exclusive?]. But the dirty secret you're uncovering is this: you can have it all, as long as you are willing to compromise, which is only another way of saying, as long as you are willing to live in the real world.

I think we are sometimes too precious with Art, as if it has to be created in a temple, and we must be its chaste supplicants, devout and unencumbered by the vagaries of common living, like having a family. Philadelphia has a brutish, blue-collar streak that says, "I got your Art right here!" before poking you in the ribs. Philadelphia puts Art next to Finance and Medicine and Law and says, "We need alla youse, so no addeetude." A whole and healthy actor is a paradox embodied, a mix of Mamet and Bates: supremely practical and deeply spiritual. This is a mark of genius—the ability to simultaneously embrace both sides of the paradox. Unfortunately, many people in the theater are invested in choosing sides.

In making it possible to be a citizen-artist, Philadelphia fulfills Stanislavsky's dream of pulling actors up from the dregs and making us full members of society: less exalted, more common, but more empowered, and more respected. Philadelphia was different thirty years ago, but something is afoot here now, something that was missing when I was in my prime.

---

[39]Quakers are guided not by edicts or directives from an authoritative body, but rather by "queries": searching questions meant to help the questioned unearth the truth.

There is an artistic gathering here, a foment. Walk through Old City on the first Friday of each month and marvel at the galleries. Count all the theaters (large and small), concert halls and museums—you'll see what I mean. But I think you already do. Philadelphia (and I include the suburbs surrounding it) is the City of Art.

But New York—ah, New York. Who am I to tell anyone, much less a talented young artist like you to leave the thrill and promise of that "insanity of light"— a phrase from an earlier letter of yours which I cherish. Here's what I know with certainty: it is much better to chart your own course than to have others do it for you. You win when you do so, not lose. And New York isn't going anywhere. You can always return. See the long view. You are an artist now and forever, and you will be wherever you settle.

So sit quietly, in any of your meetings, and listen. In the glow of the Spirit you will feel the answer.

Love,
Alice

[excerpt from *Romeo Geriatric*, created by Moveable Feast Theatre under the direction of Andrew Fallon]

Juliet/Alice alone in her room on her bed.

Juliet/Alice
Gallop apace, you fiery-footed steeds,
Towards Phoebus' lodging: such a wagoner
As Phaethon would whip you to the west,
And bring in cloudy night immediately.
Spread thy close curtain, love-performing night,
That runaway's eyes may wink and Romeo
Leap to these arms, untalk'd of and unseen.
Lovers can see to do their amorous rites
By their own beauties; or, if love be blind,
It best agrees with night. Come, civil night,
Thou sober-suited matron, all in black,
And learn me how to lose a winning match,
Play'd for a pair of stainless maidenhoods:
Hood my unmann'd blood, bating in my cheeks,
With thy black mantle; till strange love, grown bold,
Think true love acted simple modesty.
Come, night; come, Romeo; come, thou day in night;
For thou wilt lie upon the wings of night
Whiter than new snow on a raven's back.
Come, gentle night, come, loving, black-brow'd night,
Give me my Romeo; and, when he shall die,
Take him and cut him out in little stars,
And he will make the face of heaven so fine
That all the world will be in love with night
And pay no worship to the garish sun.
O, I have bought the mansion of a love,
But not possess'd it, and, though I am sold,
Not yet enjoy'd: so tedious is this day
As is the night before some festival
To an impatient child that hath new robes
And may not wear them.

Enter Edith.

Edith

What were you doing?

Alice

Nothing. Just remembering something.

Edith

Did you hear about Sam?

Alice

What about Sam?

Edith

In the hospital. Took him this morning. Ambulance, sirens, the whole thing. Got any crackers?

Alice

You know where. (*Edith gets crackers. She sits and eats.*) I like Sam.

Edith

Well I know, that's why I came to tell you. (*Pause*) It looks bad.

Alice

Oh Sam. (*Maya enters.*) Now, nurse, what news? Ay me! what news? why dost thou wring thy hands?

Nurse/Maya

Ah, well-a-day! He's dead, he's dead, he's dead!
We are undone, lady, we are undone!
Alack the day! He's gone, he's kill'd, he's dead!

Juliet/Alice

Can heaven be so envious?

Nurse/Maya

Romeo can,
Though heaven cannot: O Romeo, Romeo!
Who ever would have thought it? Romeo!

Juliet/Alice

What devil art thou, that dost torment me thus?
This torture should be roar'd in dismal hell.
Hath Romeo slain himself? say thou but 'I,'
And that bare vowel 'I shall poison more
Than the death-darting eye of cockatrice.

Nurse/Maya

I saw the wound, I saw it with mine eyes,—
God save the mark!—here on his manly breast:
A piteous corse, a bloody piteous corse;
Pale, pale as ashes, all bedaub'd in blood,
All in gore-blood; I swounded at the sight.

Juliet/Alice

O, break, my heart! poor bankrupt, break at once!
To prison, eyes, ne'er look on liberty,
Vile earth, to earth resign; end motion here;
And thou and Romeo press one heavy bier.

Edith

Easy does it, Alice. She's not talking about Sam.

Nurse/Maya

Here's your medication (*Alice takes pills*).
O Tybalt, Tybalt, the best friend I had
O courteous Tybalt! honest gentleman
That ever I should live to see thee dead.

Juliet/Alice
What storm is this that blows so contrary?
Is Romeo slaughter'd, and is Tybalt dead?
My dear-loved cousin, and my dearer lord?
Then, dreadful trumpet, sound the general doom!
For who is living, if those two are gone?

Edith
Ernie died yesterday. Sam's leaving tomorrow.

Nurse/Maya
Tybalt is gone, and Romeo banished;

Edith
They're taking Sam back home. To California. There's nothing else they can do for him. He should be with his family. He's leaving tomorrow.

Nurse/Maya
There's no trust,
No faith, no honesty in men; all perjured,
All forsworn, all naught, all dissemblers.
These griefs, these woes, these sorrows make me old.
Shame come to Romeo!

Juliet/Alice
Blister'd be thy tongue
For such a wish! he was not born to shame:
Upon his brow shame is ashamed to sit;
For 'tis a throne where honour may be crown'd
Sole monarch of the universal earth.

Edith
Sam's coming back here in a bit to collect his things.

Nurse/Maya

[Stay in] your chamber: I'll find Romeo
To comfort you: I wot well where he is.
Hark ye, your Romeo will be here at night:

Juliet/Alice

O, find him! give this ring to my true knight,
And bid him come to take his last farewell.
Exit Maya.

Edith

I'm so sorry, dear.
End scene.

[from the *Philadelphia City Paper*, August 4th, 2005]

Artbeat

For an arts reporter, the only virtue of staying in Philadelphia during one of its insufferable summers is the chance to see some of the weird stuff that gets performed around town, stuff that might not cut the mustard during the season. Usually you stumble upon something that makes you go "Huh." If you're lucky, you stumble upon something that makes you go "Wow." Last weekend I got lucky.

Moveable Feast describes itself as a "theater collective" from New York. They're in residence at The University of The Arts putting the finishing touches on *Dust*—an original piece weaving together the 9/11 attacks with myths from both classical and tribal sources, to be presented at Christ Church during the Philly Fringe next month. But it seems that wasn't enough for them, so under the guidance of Feast member Andrew Fallon, they created *Romeo Geriatric* this summer, as well. I saw a presentation of it at The Playground last Saturday night.

First, the background: Mr. Fallon's former drama teacher lives at an assisted-living situation in Swarthmore called The Quad. She is the incomparable Alice Jones, Philadelphia native and formally of the Wallingford Friends' School. She and Andrew began a correspondence which led to an investigation this summer of Shakespeare's *Romeo and Juliet*, throwing together interested older folks from The Quad with the Feasties (as they call themselves), adding original text about growing old, and giving the young roles to old folks and the old roles to young folks. Got that?

The result is an astonishing hour-long theatrical journey touching on love, loss, aging, death, alienation, and community. Ms. Jones plays Juliet. The idea of an old woman doing so seems grotesque at first glance, but through Ms. Jones the effect is incandescent. She is as full of passion and longing as any twenty-four-year old I've seen play this role, and clearly a very skilled actor. But with the dignity of her age and experience she acts as a kind of ironic, almost comic foil to Shakespeare's florid poetry. The irony vanishes however at the balcony scene, played between her and Samuel Collett as Romeo. The juxtaposition of this most beautiful love poetry coming from the mouths of septuagenarians is almost too much to bear, staged very simply and performed as it is: not as old people trying to be young again, but as old people living fully in a love deep enough to admit age. Scaling the wall becomes getting up and out of the wheelchair so he can hold her. Wasn't a dry eye anywhere.

And funny! Mr. Collett is joined by Ernest Globisch (Mercutio) and Walter Harmon (Benvolio) for some bawdiness at the expense of the Nurse (Maya Pelli), and the piece begins with a street battle in the "lounge of The Quad" using walkers, wheelchairs, and canes. Not all of it works of course, and Mr. Fallon is fortunate to have a couple of accomplished elderly amateurs among a group of, well, elderly amateurs. The Feasties (Ms. Pelli as The Nurse/Nurse, Ed Brooks as The Friar/Doctor, Kate O'Shannon as Lady Capulet/Doctor/Receptionist and Kamran Elihinia as an over-the-top Prince/Narrator/ Interviewer) generally acquit themselves well.

Sometimes the spirit and intent of a piece of theater can overcome its short-comings. Such is the case with *Romeo Geriatric*. Especially in Alice Jones' heart-felt performance, we are reminded to our shame of all the ways we marginalize the elderly. Pity Moveable Feast has no plans to present it again, otherwise you could get lucky too. You'll just have wait for *Dust*.

Jara Cimrman

[block script in red ballpoint pen on Postcard, image of Statue of Liberty on reverse]

8/15/05

To: The incomparable Alice Jones! Getting some stuff from NYC before moving in w/Maya. Gave TAG notice. Found suitable garret in Center City. Extending sublet for 1 year + teaching at UArts + Wilma Theatre in Philly. What the hell, see where the Big Hand is taking me, right? See you in coupla weeks! Andy PS: Please be in *Dust*. PPS: I love you.

Fall into Winter

F A I T H

This is the most personal section of the book, and the one in which Andy and I struggled the most about which documents to include and which not to. There were letters and e-mail between him and me, and between him and his father, which will remain unpublished, as they had much to do with the past, Andy's childhood, and David's and my divorce. We felt that including that correspondence would steer the focus away from his relationship with Alice, and the issues he was confronting during these four months. Suffice to say that there was great and painful personal growth for the three of us that we couldn't make room to represent here. We have included the documents that seemed the most germane to Andy's journey. Finally, I realized that this book itself, and the process of working on it with Andy, was more healing for Andy and me than any letter could represent.

—L.E.B.

[final page of *Dust*, created by Moveable Feast Theatre Company]

Music: Radiohead "Let Down"

Three in the air, two firemen below, standing, reaching up as if to catch.

Slide projections: William Blake's angels

Angel: Of course, it was act of hubris to fly at all. Look at Icarus. Soaring toward the sun. Wings melting in the heat.

Three in the air descend in "slow motion." Tumbling effect in harnesses. Fireman lean towards two closest.

Angel: Flying was an affront to God.

Firemen catch two falling. Embrace in pieta poses. Third reveals toy jet plane

Voice Over: Then the Angels grew wings. The wings were man's longing.

Firemen click into harnesses. They are lifted just off the ground: two and two hover in suspended "pieta."

Voice Over: Longing to be closer to God.
One with airplane lands, un-clicks from harness.

Music (crossfade): Ricki Lee Jones "Horses"

Slide projections: random photos of human faces.

Boy with airplane "flies" it towards the two, six-foot Styrofoam towers. Boy "flies" plane around the towers, enjoying it. He inadvertently bumps a tower with his elbow. It starts to fall. The boy drops the airplane and catches the tower.

Boy: Sorry.

Boy tries putting tower back in place, but it keeps tipping over. A girl comes onstage and watches. Boy keeps catching tipping towers, girl joins him. They move to the music and make a kind of dance catching the towers. Then they each hold a tower in a "pieta," directly below the hovering pairs.

End.

[script in black fountain pen on embossed stationery, "The Quad, Swarthmore, Pennsylvania" printed on the top of each page]

September 7th, 2005

Dear Andy,

Thanks to you and the Feasties for having me at rehearsal. That Church will be sued shortly for not having handicapped access to the upper floors of its rectory. Though being carried in my wheelchair up three flights of stairs by [unclear: strapping?] young men was an unexpected excitement.

You are working together in the most marvelous way. Kamran is a gifted director. I can only surmise that it is his familiarity with you all, his bond to you, which makes him so adept at both challenging you to excel and sensing just what each of you needs in tricky moments. I think we have lost something with our itinerant [unclear: lifestyle?] in the theater. All the great companies in history were ones in which the artists worked together over time, and their collaboration was life-collaboration. I'm convinced part of Shakespeare's genius came from the fact of his writing for his friends. When the character Hamlet began [unclear: walking or wandering] through his mind, Richard Burbage was wearing the costume, and Richard's gifts are present in Hamlet's words. Now we are thrown together with strangers over and over, contributing to our [unclear: defensiveness or divisiveness], our attachment to "methods" and our wounded clinging to the production calendar, necessarily timed for self-destruction. How I have longed for artistic relationships that last. The only one I had was with WFS, and even then, you all kept graduating!

The most effective aspect of <u>Dust</u> is, in my opinion, the images you have created. The [unclear: suspension?] of actors in space with those ropes and pullies is astonishing. The way you are using spatial relationships is powerful, deeply affecting. And the final image of you as the young boy playing with airplanes and towers is devastating. You saw the effect it had on me. Where the piece goes off the rails, I think, is with the text (particularly the original sections) and with the accompanying music and sound. I found the "real life" vignettes oddly offensive. If you take a nation's greatest tragedy and use it as the [illegible] for a work of art, you'd better be up to the task. I think you need a real playwright to work on these bits. They seem [illegible] shallow, sometimes melodramatic and I worry they do not honor the dead. This is the challenge you face—you are not working [illegible], a fact that everyone will have strong feelings about.

Also, the music and sound is just too loud. It overwhelms, it seems to want to compensate for weaknesses in other areas.

But do not let my blunt criticism deter you. As Wilde says, if one has something unpleasant to say, one should be candid. If you find my notes sound, well, you have several days to work. If not, you may write me off as an old fuddy-duddy. My opinions pale next to the [*unclear: courage?*] of young artists making art. You all are a force of nature, no less than the stubborn shoot bursting through the cold ground in March. The art is yours now so much more than mine. You are going one way and I am going the other.

I won't be coming to see it performed. I must tell you that it took me a full two days to recover from my trip [*illegible*] to watch you rehearse. But do come to the Quad and bring Maya and tell me how it went with an audience. I will be with you in the Spirit.

Love,
Alice

[black felt-tip pen on yellow legal pad]

9/12/05

Dear Alice,
      How does an actor get a "reputation??" And why is that held
over my head like a threat?? And what the hell does it mean??
      Kamran took me aside after a testy note session and told me
that I was in danger of "earning a reputation."
      "Reputation of what?" I asked.
      You know. You're difficult.
      How am I difficult?
      You're being defiant, inflexible.
      Jesus! I'm just asking questions!
      There's no time for questions.
      Then we should stop rehearsing.
      You know, you're in danger of earning a reputation.
      How's that for your robust collaboration? I was sullen and
moody the rest of the night, thinking about this encounter,
thinking about your critical notes. Alice, your timing sucks. Don't
you get it that your opinion matters more to me than almost any
other? I guess not, otherwise why would you sabotage me with your
thoughts about *Dust* being offensive—two days before we open
?!?! By the way, we performed it in New York where the shit happened and no one seemed terribly offended.
      We open at the Fringe tomorrow (well tonight, actually), it's 2:14
a.m. I'm filled with dread. This thing that I used to believe in so
much has suddenly become unreliable. I haven't seen Dr. Kayne in
over a month. She's given me a list of people to see in Philly. ~~I want
to tell her to just go~~ She wants me to explore something called
Psychodrama. I thought she was joking. ~~Like I'm some sort of
fucking guinea pig~~ I haven't been to a meeting in over a week.
      I don't know what I'm doing here in this city. Philly seems so
small and stupid to me now. It's like Newark only further away. I
feel disconnected from my life—like I'm floating over it, watching
myself like I'm some other person. The sudden emotional rushes are
back, but this time it's not joy and grief—it's panic. I'll be walking
along the sidewalk and suddenly feel overcome with fear. Maybe

AND WHAT IS
THE DEAL WITH
THE WEATHER
HERE? IT'S HELL

that's what happened to me in rehearsal the other night. It happened again when I got home tonight. I scared Maya. I had to pace around clutching a pillow to my chest, hyperventilating, occasionally moaning like a wounded animal. I thought I was getting better, but I feel more crazy than ever.

~~Fuck him and his reputation bullshit! How dare he? He doesn't know me well enough to pull shit like that on me! He just couldn't answer my questions! He had no answers, he couldn't admit it, so he turned on me, the miserable insecure little shit. Fuck him, I'll take his reputation any day.~~

You know what it is? It had been going so well. We were working together seamlessly. And then we had this really hard rehearsal. I wasn't the only one having trouble. Kate got so frustrated with her harness she threw it across the room and stormed out. We had to wait a half hour while she smoked enough cigarettes to calm down and keep working. It was just a fucked up night—it felt like a betrayal.

Enough. I miss you. Maya misses you. We'll be out to see you soon.

Love,
Andy

PS: I just realized it. Yesterday was 9/11. How did none of us acknowledge that? How could we have been so blind?

[e-mail to Andy 9/12/05]

andy yo: forget about the other night. whatever. too much stress. know what? the show belongs to you guys now (again). let's just kick ass and not look back. peace kam.

[script in black fountain pen on embossed stationery, "The Quad, Swarthmore, Pennsylvania" printed on the top of each page]

Sept. 14, 2005

Dear Andy,

Feeling very weak today. Hope you broke both legs upon opening.

A "reputation" is like gossip. One must always consider the source. Frequently the source is entirely [*illegible*]. Truth is between two involved—what <u>happened</u>? Reputation is sometimes an act of vengeance from someone without the guts to tell it to you straight. Rumor, innuendo, poison.

Wish they didn't matter. They do. You create your own legacy. Esp. if you stay in one place, folks get to know you. Pick your fights carefully. Some matter, some don't. For which will you [*unclear: risk?*] a "reputation?"

Don't come weekend. I'm getting a transfusion tomorrow, I'll [*illegible*] back. Next week better.

Love,
Alice.

PS: Sorry about my timing. But thicken your skin, my boy!

&

[handwritten note on stationery "Mackenzie-Fallon, San Francisco." Enclosed was a check dated September 16th to Andy for $1,000]

Hey Buddy—Miss you a <u>lot</u>. Damn it, I'm coming for Christmas—hell or high water! Mom tells me you're moving. Enclosed to help with expenses. I love you. Dad.

Dust—* [one star out of five]
Moveable Feast Theatre

Ostensibly a kind of memorial-in-performance to the events of 9/11/2001, *Dust* unfortunately has the opposite effect. Loud, clumsy and obtuse, *Dust* manages to provoke anguish but of the entirely wrong kind. With all the grace and accomplishment of a high-school senior project, this piece weaves together myths with invented scenes from that terrible day. You avert your eyes, but more out of shame and embarrassment for the performers than as the result of any profound or artistic point being made.

Performed in and around a kind of giant jungle gym, the actors (and I use that term advisedly) are frequently winched into the air using harnesses and an elaborate block and tackle scheme. The whole thing is so cumbersome it distracts from the performance. But in this case that's not an entirely bad thing.

The invented scenes from inside the towers and airplanes have all the originality of a TV movie of the week. The acting is just bad: either robotic or melodramatic. The myths used range from the incomprehensible (something about flying Hindu elephants) to the obvious (Icarus finally appears at the end—what a surprise).

And finally one has to ask: What's the point? Are we being asked to sit through this so that we can watch these youngsters cavort in their playground at the expense of 3,000 dead? Bad theater is one thing and occasionally forgivable, but bad theater, which pretends to be "important," is obnoxious. The company responsible for *Dust* is called Moveable Feast. One hopes that next time they will dine in.

Ryan Desmond

[note card with black and white photo of a very wet cat on the front, hand written in blue ballpoint pen]

9/20

Dear Barbara,

Just following up to see if there might be a job for me at Haverford next semester. And to say again how very cool it was to study with you last summer. I'm using so much of what we shared together in my UArts class—and it feels like it's mine!

Dust continues but we got scragged in the Inky. Oh well. Hope you'll check it out anyway. Runs through the end of next week.

Love,
Andy

[Printed in Times New Roman. Fearing her handwriting was becoming illegible, Alice told Andy later that she dictated this letter to Edith Murphy, who had a computer, and that Edith was responsible for the joke mentioned at the end of the letter. She sent it to the *Philadelphia Inquirer*. It was never published. She also sent a copy to Andy]

September 22, 2005

Dear Sirs,

I have been reading your newspaper for over fifty years now, and I have found it generally sound. The one glaring exception is your arts and cultural coverage—particularly your reviews. I had long ago given up reading them, having found them to be nothing more than long-winded opinion pieces written by persons whose opinions I have no reason to respect at all. But recently some friends of mine performed at the Philadelphia Fringe Festival, and so I held my nose and read your review of their piece, *Dust*. Ordinarily, when one encounters something odious, one passes by, since lingering with it has the effect of extending the irritation. And yet, Mr. Desmond's review of *Dust* is odiousness of the most deplorable kind, and so must be dealt with.

My disclaimer is that I worked with this company of actors this summer. But lest you think that fact denies me objectivity, consider this: I saw a rehearsal of *Dust* and was critical of it. What I told them was that the execution of the piece was faulty, that they needed a playwright to fashion scenes with real integrity, and that it all felt a bit overwrought to me. But I also told them they managed to create moments of searing beauty—beauty of the kind that transforms you, for it takes grief and releases it, making room for healing to begin. Young artists like these doing brave work face extraordinary challenges and they need to be supported, yes, even when what they make is wanting, and especially when they reach high, as Moveable Feast does with *Dust*.

Whether the editors of this newspaper or Mr. Desmond like it or not, the fact is this: your newspaper is part of the grand creative process of art-making in this city. There is an important role for critics to play in this process, but your newspaper hasn't found it yet. For years, you have sat on the outside of that process like a spoiled child with delusions of grandeur, passing judgments on what you see as if those judgments have any objective authority. They do not and they never have. There is no such thing as "good" or "bad" art, there is only the work itself and one's subjective response to it. Friends of mine who attended opening night of *Dust* reported that they and many others wept at the end. One wonders why that subjective response didn't make it into your review. But I forget. Mr. Desmond, who seems to have not liked *Dust* very much, is King Baby, and only his subjective response matters.

Perhaps next time he sees a play he doesn't like, rather than having a tantrum in print about it, he might say something intelligent and helpful about how the piece in question might improve. He might wipe his tears away, get down from his highchair, grow up and join the dance. Rather than just emitting his opinions, one hopes he will enjoy being a part of something bigger: the grand creative process I mentioned before. After all, there's an important joke about opinions, and the punch line goes like this: everyone has one.

Alice Jones
Wallingford, PA

[Times New Roman on plain white paper]

September 29th, 2005

Dear Alice,

    I'm Andy's mother and I just wanted to write and say thanks for everything you're doing for him. We met at *Romeo Geriatric*—don't know if you remember or not.

    He also told me that your health has become an issue, and I wanted you to know that we—his Massachusetts family—are all thinking of you. You have helped him so much this year, during this transition in his life. If there's anything we can do, please do let us know.

Your fan from afar!
Linda Berkowitz

PS: When you knew me before in the '80s I was Linda Fallon, then Linda Emlin.

[script in black fountain pen on embossed stationery, "The Quad, Swarthmore, Pennsylvania" printed on the top of each page]

October 6th, 2005

Dear Linda,

It's not my health that's an issue, it's my death, which I sense is near. You know it's a bad sign when your doctors start to talk about "keeping you [*unclear: comfortable?*]" But thank you for your letter. Next time though, I will be glad if you wrote with your hand.

Thoughts are fine, but I would prefer that you hold me in the Light. Thoughts are what secular people do who need spiritual expression and haven't acknowledged their own yet. You were raised a Quaker—I know your parents. I used to visit them at Newtown Square Meeting, which alas has been laid down.[40] Our Society is fighting for it's survival.

So find a quiet place and sit there. Imagine a warm and welcoming Light. Put me in it. I will be grateful.

Yours,
Alice Jones

PS: It's not my relationship to Andy that matters so much anymore. It's yours.

---

[40]When a meeting no longer has enough members to sustain it, the Quarter it is in—a group of nearby meetings—may decide to close the meeting in question (lay it down).

Dear Dad—Sorry it's taken me a while to get back to you. Things have been really busy here. Maya and I moved in together, I was in a play called *Dust* and I'm teaching at the University of the Arts here in Philly. I'm also auditioning for plays.

I know you think I'm crazy leaving New York, but there was nothing there for me anymore. You have the normal attitude most people have about being an actor—it means going to New York or Los Angeles. I had no idea how powerful this message was until I tried to leave. It felt like I was committing an act of treason. It felt like I was betraying some promise I made to myself, to my family, to my art—that I was gonna stick it out no matter what. But stick it out for what?

See Dad, there are some very specific reasons to be an actor in NYC or LA:

1. you like those cities and you like living there
2. you want to act in the theater communities of those cities
3. you want to be in movies and TV

Those are the only reasons I can think of to be there. I can answer no to reasons 1 and 2.

#3 is trickier. Of course I want to be in a fabulous movie or TV show and make a gazillion dollars and go to swanky restaurants. But I understand now that it's less of a career goal and more of a fantasy for me—like hoping that some day I'll bed Uma Thurman. How much misery and shit does a person have to put up with for the sake of a fantasy? Maybe some day Uma and I will meet on a Hawaiian island and one thing will lead to another, but I'm sure as hell not going to start swimming across the Pacific with a pack of rubbers strapped to my back, which is sort of what my life in NYC was feeling like. I was drowning.

Like all Dads, you're worried about my career. Well, it's simple in theory—I want to be a working actor. But I also want to have a home, and just recently I realized that I really, really want to have a family—my own family, the boring normal kind. So I've expanded what it means to be a working actor. I need to put things in place to make this family goal come true. I will always act. Sometimes I'll get paid for it more than other times. But added to that now is a genuine fascination with teaching acting, which I've discovered is an oxymoron, but never mind. In teaching I get to work in the field I love, and have a kind of job security that might, *might* support a family. In order to have a shot at this new life I'm imagining, I need a partner, a place to live and a community which supports me. In Philly I found all three.

You see, the idea that a person can make a living being an actor alone is complete bullshit. It has been for a long time. But many of us cling to it, hoping that through the force of our will and some luck we will be able to play characters for the rest of out lives and be paid for it. This is true for maybe 5% of all actors in America—A- and B-list movie and TV stars. The other 95% of us will always need to do something else in addition to acting to make ends meet. What that something else is, and how often we have to do it depends on a lot of variables. But I have chosen that something else—teaching—and I have chosen not to see it as a defeat, or even a compromise, but a celebration.

I hope you can come here some day and witness that celebration in person. In all honesty, I really don't want to come to San Francisco. The memories are still too painful. Come East and bring Sharon and the boys. Then you can meet Maya and see the little nest we've built on Camac Street. I can take you to The Last Drop and you can meet the amazing people we hang out with who are making art in this city. Maybe we can see a show. If you're here during the week, you can come to the University of the Arts, and meet my students there.

Is Philadelphia so special? I think so. But the actors in Seattle don't, or Chicago, or Atlanta, or Austin, or Boston, or Denver, or Santa Fe. I hear San Fran has a sweet artistic vibe. There is a New Paradigm for the actor and it is growing in the regions, where actors are settling down and becoming citizens. The Citizen-Actor. It's the next big thing.

New York was a stop along my way here. It was my necessary taste of the gypsy paradigm. I was a transient there, flailing and wounded, dancing for spare change thrown by passers by, just enough to get me to the next drink. It was an insidious manifestation of my childhood wound: unconnected, sad, performing in order to gain the love I thought would vanish unless I kept performing. Looking back, there was no way I could ever have had a healthy relationship to that city. But that's me. I left some friends there who love it and are doing fine. They have a plan. More power to them.

I crashed and burned there, but a beautiful bird rose from the ashes, exotic and essential, shining in all colors. That bird took me here and showed me how build a nest.

In my New Paradigm I am multi-faceted. I am a Quaker disco ball, reflecting Divine Light in many directions at once. I teach, and it is my joy to do so. My acting is refreshed and challenged by my encounters with my students, who ask the basic questions, the ones that are the hardest to answer. I discover things as an actor and I bring these discoveries to my students. Case in point: I was recently in a show that got panned in the papers. We re-grouped and re-committed ourselves to that project, and I learned about an actor's priorities. We serve an audience, and if we are convinced of that success, nothing else (like bad reviews) matters. My students read those reviews and saw that show. The discussions we had about it all were the stuff great education is made of.

The Citizen Actor is linked to the community he serves. The school I teach at not only tolerates my acting, but encourages it. They are committed to me as a teaching artist, and they understand the value of my work in the field, the same way a biologist's research is supported, or an historian's articles. The people I work with in this city have worked with each other for years, and that longevity of relationship is a source of pride. The community I serve has grown up with a large company of local actors, and looks forward to recognizing them in a play, remembering them from one they saw last year and marveling at the transformation. I live next door to the people I act for. I bump into them in the grocery store. We attend political rallies and see movies together. We are connected.

This huge life-change has been made possible by some important, fundamental things. I stopped drinking and I started going to meetings. Even though I haven't been to one in a while, it has made everything else possible. So please, no more quaint comments about "going off the stuff." When you visit, I'll tell you all about it face to face. I started seeing a shrink (Dr. Kayne). I don't think you ever knew how fucked up and miserable I was in NYC. Nobody did, because I was too ashamed to admit it. I needed a place to go where I was the subject and my issues were front and center. It was only through my work with Dr. Kayne that I began to untangle the knots from my childhood. I have Mom to thank for that. She set me up with her. And then there's Alice Jones, my drama teacher from WFS. In a moment of deep despair I wrote to her last December. Her letters to me and our subsequent reconnection have inspired me. You may not "get" this next bit, but she has been my spirit-guide. I can't conceive of doing any of the things I've described to you in this (epic) e-mail without Alice in the background. Through her, I began to explore Quakerism as a possible home for my budding spiritual life.

By now, you're probably asking yourself, Why is he telling me all this. Isn't it obvious Dad? I want you back in my life. But you need to know what my life is like first. I don't know how this will be possible, with us living on opposite coasts. But let's start with this premise: It's not the quantity of time we spend together that matters anymore, but the quality. You have my invitation.

For the last month, your check has sat on the "altar" Maya and I have in our apartment. It's a little desk with a pretty cloth on it and some candles. We put things or images there that we wish for, or that trouble us. A picture of Alice, who is ill, is on the altar. Several brochures of local theater companies announcing their seasons are on the altar too. So is my Barry Bonds bobble-head doll (spirituality must have a sense of humor!). Sometimes, before bed, one or both of us will go in there and light a candle and just sit there for a while. So I've been sitting in front of your check for a while, and I've decided to deposit it. It is going to pay for a new kind of therapy I'm exploring, so you see Dad, you will be a part of my recovery, my growth, my incarnation. You are feeding that glorious bird.

In the place of your check, I'm putting a picture of you and Mom on the altar. It's from when you were married and happy. I don't know how I acquired this photograph, but you have your arm around her and you're both smiling like you're about to bust out laughing. You're both leaning against a railing with a body of water behind you (Lake Michigan?), and Mom's hair is all crazy. It goes on the altar not because I want what I cannot have, but because it reminds me that I was born in love, and that maybe someday I will pass that love along.

I have my ups and downs. It's up now. Say hi to Sharon, Danny, and James for me. Tell them Big Brother Andy wants to wrestle!

Love,
Andy

[hand written in black fountain pen, "Haverford College, Department of Fine &
Performing Arts" embossed on the top of each page]

October 12th, 2005

Dear Andy,

Got your note—thanks. Unfortunately no, there are no openings for adjunct
faculty next spring. But it sounds like your life is rich and getting richer—
teaching and performing all together, living the life you want to live. What an
accomplishment!

Sadly, I never got to see Dust. My loss for sure. About the review. I've been
re-reading a book I turn to in times of spiritual turmoil, a state I find myself in
as I prepare to hand in my application for tenure. It's called Letters to a Young
Poet and it's by the Czech poet Ranier Maria Rilke (he's considered German
because that's the language he wrote in, but he was born and raised in Prague).
For reasons I can't quite explain, I've been thinking of you as I've been reading
this little book over the last few weeks. Here's what he tells the Young Poet
about criticism:

"Read as little as possible of aesthetic criticism—such things are either par-
tisan views, petrified and grown senseless in their lifeless induration, or they are
clever quibblings in which today one view wins and tomorrow the opposite.
Works of art are of an infinite loneliness and with nothing so little to be reached
as with criticism. Only love can grasp and hold and be just toward them."

Rilke spends a great deal of time in these letters writing about solitude, loneliness and sadness. I think the Young Poet writing to him was having a rough go
of it. Maybe that's why I'm thinking of you. I know how tough it is when you
begin, and the task at hand—to be an artist in the world—seems absurd and
impossible. Rilke reminds us that the difficult feelings we experience as artists
are not signs that we are failing, quite the opposite, they are assurances that we
have found the way. Rilke was 28 when he wrote these letters. Maybe that's
another reason I'm thinking of you.

Good luck and stay in touch,
Barbara Lewis

[note left for Maya on the kitchen table, October 15th, 2005, in pencil on yellow legal pad]

IS THIS ABOUT US?

"Where I create I am true, and I want to find the strength to build my life wholly upon this truth, upon this infinite simplicity and joy that is sometimes given me . . . But how shall I begin?"
AND
"In one creative thought a thousand forgotten nights of love revive, filling it with sublimity and exaltation. And those who come together in the night and are entwined in rocking delight do an earnest work and gather sweetnesses, gather depth and strength for the song of some coming poet, who will arise to speak of ecstasies beyond telling."

From the awesome book Barbara Lewis turned me on to: Rilke's "Letters to the Young Poet." Sat here in the morning light while you were sleeping and read it and cried. Left it here for you. Enjoy your day—see you after class.

Huge Love—
A.

[script in gold ink on maroon hand-made paper]

October 15th

Dear Alice,

Just keeping myself busy during some "down time." Andy gave me this paper-making kit for my birthday and I LOVE IT! See all the stuff in the paper? It's ground up lavender and if you sniff the paper it smells WONDERFUL. I know how you love letters and I thought you'd enjoy a whole new sensory experience in letter reading . . .

Andy left me this book this morning called <u>Letters to a Young Poet</u> by Rilke. Do you know it? It's making me think of you—so much about stillness and listening. Seems kinda Quaker to me . . . but that's not what I really want to tell you about.

I saw an amazing play last week. Do you know who Bill Irwin is? He's an extraordinary clown. More exactly, he's a great theater artist who makes theater using the performance "language" of clown and vaudeville (follow that?) Anyway, he made a piece recently about a vaudeville clown who was a sensation in New York right after the civil war. Guess what this man's name was? GEORGE FOX! I was astonished! I've been trying to get in touch with Irwin to find out if he knows of any connection between this man and the founder of Quakerism.

George Fox the clown's greatest achievement was a piece he made called "Humpty Dumpty"—are you laughing yet?—in which he pops out of a big egg and then gets into all kinds of trouble. Irwin was brilliant in it, sweet and vulnerable and exquisitely skilled. It's the kind of work I aspire to. And the story he told about this man's life was so moving. He was robbed by the theater managers and died dissolute.

So George Fox has come to us twice. First as the founder of the Religious Society of Friends and then as the clown who made Humpty Dumpty a household name. Thought you should know. There is some Divine Paradox at work here I know you'll appreciate.

The Feasties are gone and life seems a little empty without them. I wish them all so much happiness and success. I love those guys. You'll never know how much your letter in defense of <u>Dust</u> meant to us, even though the jerks wouldn't publish it. We all got drunk at The Plough and The Stars (except Andy!) and Kamran did a very loud and expressive reading of it from atop his bar stool.

It's strange. Usually when something ends I panic. But here I am puttering around my apartment waiting for Andy to get home from teaching. Making paper and writing you a letter. And feeling just fine. My life is a blessing.

Pig Iron is doing a benefit Halloween night and I will be riding a unicycle in a tutu and singing dirty songs. Any chance you could come?

Love,
Maya

Hey Mom—

Okay—Psychodrama update. First of all, most practitioners don't call it Psychodrama anymore because that term has been co-opted to mean a neurotic, theatrical outburst. While this kind of therapy can engender these, it's not an association people like, so they call it Drama Therapy more often. I've been going once a week since mid-September.

The main Dude, the Therapist in our group, is called the Director. His name is Phil Tronceletti and he's been working as a Drama Therapist for 10 years. He has a Master's in Clinical Psychology from Yale. The program I'm in is sponsored by U Penn. When I interviewed with him (all participants have to be accepted into the group, it's like a cross between a job interview and psychotherapy session) he learned a lot about my issues. He also gave me the Brief History of Psychodrama. We meet with him once a month individually and once a week as a group, in a big carpeted room with these large, semi-soft square and rectangular building blocks we can build things with.

Back in Vienna in the 1920s, a Swiss guy named J.R. Moreno wanted to start a theater group based on what we now call Improvisation: actors creating theater spontaneously without a script. But he kept losing his best actors to "legit" acting gigs. He kept at it though, and he gradually noticed a psychotherapeutic aspect to the work with the enthusiasts who stayed. Then his goals shifted from the artistic to the therapeutic. It was really a shift in emphasis: the creativity remains, but public performance is never the goal.

Over the years there have been ins and outs, different kinds of Drama Therapy invented, splinter groups and infighting. But what Tronceletti is doing is pretty close to what Moreno ended up with. So: Tronceletti is the "director." The person at the center of each session's exploration is called the "protagonist." The rest of the class are "auxiliary egos" who participate in the protagonist's improvisation. Each session has three parts:

- A warm-up, which uses vocal and physical exercises and guided discussion to bring the group's attention to one person or one idea. Out of the warm-up, a protagonist volunteers.
- The action, in which the protagonist sets the stage and designs, with the aid of the director, an improvisation around a central concern of his. Guided by the director, a dynamic encounter takes place between the antagonist and some source of psychic stress performed and embodied by the auxiliary egos. During the action, every member of the group is involved. Even if observing, they occasionally call out reactions to what is happening or are enlisted by the director in a variety of ways.
- Closure, in which all participants are invited to share through guided discussion their emotional reaction to the action which has just ended.

The primary goal is to create a theatrical, improvised encounter between the protagonist and the lost event or unresolved issue that haunts him, an encounter that he designs and participates in, but that is guided by the director. Dr. T does a lot of different things during the sessions. He may make the protagonist repeat an encounter several times. He may add a third character to an encounter between two. Once he asked us all to make soft moaning sounds underneath an elaborate improv in which this woman was looking for treasure. Sometimes the auxiliary egos participate in an empathetic response to the unfolding drama of each session. Dr. T will come around to us and whisper "Support her" so we shout "Go for it!" or "You can do it" when a protagonist is facing a crisis.

Here's what happened to me. You know about the check Dad sent me, and how pissed I was about it. Well I volunteered to be the protagonist and give "Dad" the check back, and tell him what he could do with it. Dr. T instructed the guy playing "Dad" to evade me, and I was not allowed to run after him. So every time I approached him he moved away. I was told to vocalize. It was frustrating. "Come here! Stay in one place, motherfucker!" I shouted. Dr. T put others in the room who were from my past. "Dad" was to hide behind them. When I bumped up against one of these people "Dad" was hiding behind, they would ask me, "Who am I?" I had to tell them who they were quickly without thinking. Then they would say, "What do you want?" And I had to explain what I wanted to say to my Dad. They were encouraged to engage in conversation with me about it, playing the role I had assigned them to the best of their ability (during the warm-up Dr. T asked me a bunch of questions about roles others might play, so they weren't completely in the dark). It was uncanny how accurate many of them were. I was allowed to move around them when I felt the conversation had run its course. You were there of course. Robby. Maya. Alice. Virginia my voice teacher from Emerson. Remember Mr. Henderson the shop teacher I had in Oakland? The one who looked out for me at that terrible school? He was there, and when I "met" him I regressed entirely to 5th grade. I wept and shouted and stamped my feet, "Get out of the way! I want to talk to Daddy!"

Then Dr. T had me meet "Dad," but Dr. T stood behind the guy playing him and whispered things for him to say to me. "Dad" said "Please keep the money. It's the only way I can love you now." I annihilated him. Dr. T had two people hold me so I could push against them while I screamed at "Dad"—just nasty outrageous stuff. Then it was over. Dr. T had "Dad" offer his hand (I was on the floor, coming out of crying, breathing hard). I took his hand and we shook.

We wrapped up and there was a lot of group support for the journey I had gone on. The whole thing lasted maybe fifteen minutes, but even as I write this it seems like I was gone for days. Dr. T asked me what I was going to do with the check. I said, "Deposit it and use it to pay for this therapy." That night I wrote Dad an e-mail and told him so.

This whole year has been about figuring out how to be a healthy actor. How to be an actor and not hurt myself through my acting. How to make acting a celebration of the good parts of me, not a repetition of my anguish. This kind of therapy is such a perfect fit. Dr. Kayne was so important, but it always felt a little lonely in there with her (maybe it was supposed to). My spiritual, creative energy is turned on by groups, and Drama Therapy uses constructs and designs I'm so familiar with. It's given me a place to work out my shit theatrically, so I don't have to work it out in rehearsal. And I love the idea that I'm helping others while I help myself. Frequently, at the wrap-up sessions, someone who had been an auxiliary ego will have a break-through based on something they participated in peripherally, or something they witnessed the protagonist go through. The woman who played you during my session was especially moved, having lost a son in Iraq. Our encounter was so intense I had to move away from it. Some sessions are frustrating and move nowhere. Mine was more explosive than others, but that was the territory I chose to explore. None of it would work if I didn't trust Dr. T implicitly, and feel really good about our group. I'm lucky that I can say yes to both of those.

Other news: I'm in a Chris Durang play for a group called Theatre Exile. There's no money in it but the people are really cool and the show is very funny. We've just started rehearsing and on the way home I had this thought. I realized that I *want* people to like me, and that this is part of my desire to act. And THAT'S OKAY. I *want* applause, laughter, admiration. I used to feel embarrassed about that, but I don't anymore. In one of his letters, Rilke talks about beauty being the longing for love manifested visually. My longing for love manifests in my performance. I want to be in love with the audience and they with me, I want an intimate embrace with them. And this longing is what my spiritual energy feels like as it shoots out of me—it's not entirely comfortable. It's an intense feeling, full of passion and vulnerability. And others feel it and sense it. Some thrill to it, and others shrink from it. But on stage it is what we call charisma, what Stanislavsky calls stage charm. It is lovelonging, and every good actor has it and should embrace it.

About a month ago, a few days after *Dust* was panned, I was walking to the theater, and this older man stopped me on the sidewalk. He looked entirely blue-collar Philly, and sounded it. "Saw the Dust play last night. I wanna shake your hand. That was a brave thing you kids did. Very powerful. Thanks." I was speechless. What was a man like that doing coming to *Dust*? I said Thank you three or four times, and as I walked away I had what Quakers call an "opening." My face burned as I thought, *he's* who I do this for, not the fucking critics, and if he likes it, then what I'm doing is good. He paid for his ticket, he stopped me on the street, he thanked me. That's the review I'll take to heart. It's like that line from Franny and Zooey about the Fat Lady: It's Christ, Christ himself, buddy.[41] I have to have faith in that man on the street.

Classes going well. Lots of thoughts about that. Another time. *Beyond Therapy* goes up around Thanksgiving. Come down with the family and feast with me and Maya?

Love you,
Andy

&

---

[41] *Franny and Zooey* by J.D. Salinger. I gave this book to Andy, who was deeply affected by it. He used a monologue from it for auditions. In it, Zooey remembers his older brother Seymore telling him about a Fat Lady in the audience that he (Seymore) imagined as Christ.

[Opening statement of Barbara Lewis's application for tenure and promotion to Associate Professor of Theatre, Haverford College. My thanks to Prof. Lewis for her permission to use it here. Submitted November 1st, 2005, the application was pending as of this printing]

Opening Statement

Why teach acting at a liberal arts institution? Within a curriculum committed to high achievement in a broad spectrum of intellectual topics, what benefit does the study of acting add? The answer to these questions involves an articulation of the very purpose of higher education, and the role that creativity should play in it. In many ways, teaching creative process—acting being one such process, painting being another—runs counter to some prevailing trends in academia. For example, creative processes can be stifled by too much emphasis on the purely intellectual, they resist conventional modes of evaluating efficacy, they are not easily described through clearly articulated syllabi. Instead, creative achievement blooms in the release of the instinctual, and each student progresses at different speeds, making uniform modes of evaluation unsuitable. One student's tiny step may be a great accomplishment while another's dazzling performance may be an act of laziness. Creative processes generally (and acting especially) are experienced, witnessed and evaluated based on the *virtues* of the artist engaged in them, rather than on objectively measurable intellectual accomplishment. This makes the teaching of acting difficult to explain intellectually. But it is precisely because of this "virtue-based" aspect that acting *should* be taught in higher education, in spite of its slippery and subjective nature. There are few other classes that use virtues as the basis for pedagogy. I am and will remain an educator who is committed to the exploration and celebration of the virtues of the actor.

Of the many virtues required of the actor, the most important is empathy. Realistic acting—one style I teach among several—demands that the actor empathize with the character. In other styles in which character empathy is not a requirement (Brechtian alienation, for example), empathy is the key to connecting to the message of the piece performed or to the actor/audience relationship. But in realistic acting, which is the "default style" of American theater, television, and film, it is the empathy for the character the student plays that is most important. Without that empathy, the student will revert to "me acting": a narcissistic system dominated by the student's experience alone.

By stressing empathy, the student's attention is turned outward. From my years of teaching acting, I have observed an empathetic "ripple effect" set off in my classes: my students begin to create close relationships to each other in the classroom, leading to the creation of a dynamic and supportive ensemble which breaks down the usual barriers of class, race, and social cliques. Empathy leads them to personalize their education in many ways. For instance, they begin to have a much deeper relationship to the books they read in other classes. Empathy engenders outward connections, connections born of feelings that link the student to what they do emotionally, and this makes what they do matter to them. My experience has shown me that when the student has a personal stake in the outcome of their assignment, the work they turn in is usually exceptional. The way I teach it, acting breeds empathy, and empathy breeds students who look for heart and meaning in everything they do.

The other virtue I wish to identify at the outset is faith. One of the hardest things a student actor learns to do is explore without knowing. Actors learn to grope; they learn to try things knowing that what they discover may be lacking in some way. They learn to embrace what Martha Graham called the "queer dissatisfaction" of the artist's exploration—ever seeking, never satisfied. The key to this kind of creative exploration is faith. Student actors must develop faith in themselves and in each other that the process of searching is a reward in itself, that it is a never-ending approach to an unattainable perfection. The "product" loses importance as the process grows more fascinating. They must also have faith in their instructor, and I am glad to point to my student evaluations as evidence that this has been true in my case. Without faith, without an abiding belief that the search is part of a higher purpose, the student will founder. In James 2:14–26, the disciple says, "faith without works is dead." The basis of my application for tenure flips that truth around. I say, work without faith is dead.

There is a spiritual nature to the actor's work, which deserves attention in the classroom. It is non-sectarian and non-dogmatic. It seeks neither conversions to nor affirmations of any belief system, but rather examines the mysterious ways human beings move each other emotionally. The issues of empathy and faith already mentioned are a part of the spiritual nature of acting, as is another, which has become important in my classes: service. The actor serves: his partner on stage, his audience, and his own spiritual calling. This exploration of faith is quite often missed in the field of actor training. Developing these artistic virtues is often trumped by the minutia of script analysis in the halls of higher education, work which bends acting to an intellectual design. In the following pages,

I will propose a course of training which de-emphasizes the intellectual in actor training, and explores the work of the actor through the virtues required, touching on the specific challenges posed by each of the courses I teach. And I will use the Quaker testimonies of Simplicity, Integrity, Community, and Equality as a framework for the spiritual exploration of my work.

[black ballpoint pen on hand-made light blue paper]

November 3rd, 2005

Dear Alice,

Sorry it's been so long. It's unbelievable how full my life is. Right after I moved here I was freaking out because I thought I'd have nothing to do. Now I can barely find time to ~~take a~~ have dinner with Maya.

I have so much to tell you about my classes. But I'm going to wait until we can see each other. My problem now is doubt. I'm just really not sure being in Philly is right for me. I'm in a show, but I feel like an outsider and I feel jittery all the time. I'm not making meetings. I feel like I jumped into this situation because I was afraid of New York, like I'm a pussy for not sticking it out, even though I know it was killing me. I wrote my Dad this long e-mail about the "New Paradigm" of the actor, the Actor Citizen, and now I feel like it's just a bunch of horseshit and we're all as desperate down here as we were up there, only the stakes aren't as high. It's like I suddenly have this sense of my life stretching out before and it's freaking me out. Doing the same ol' same ol', dum dee dum dee dum, then—holy shit! I'm 70!

So, are you okay? Maya wrote you a couple of weeks ago and we've heard nothing. You're not answering your phone (again—hello?). We're planning the pre-Thanksgiving Thanksgiving we spoke of a while back—coming out to the Quad and wining and dining you. Write or call, we want to know how you are.

We love you!
Andy

November 5, 2005

Dear Andy,

Alice has been in the hospital for the last several days. She is failing. It seems to be one of those manage-the-demise exercises. She hates it here, but there is really no other option.

She has so loved your letters, and Maya's, but is too frail to write back and will not use the phone. She can't hold the receiver to her head and she won't let anyone else do it for her. Her thoughts are a bit jumbled these days. She tried to dictate a letter to me but it was impossible. We nearly fell out over it.

She is in room 118 in Springfield Hospital. Come by soon. Yours, Edith Murphy

[blue ballpoint pen on note card, ink drawing of Swarthmoor Hall, England, on the cover]

Nov. 5th, '05

Dear Andy,

Alice has been in the hospital for the last several days. She is failing. It seems to be one of those manage-the-demise exercises. She hates it here, but there is really no other option.

She has so loved your letters, and Maya's, but is too frail to write back and will not use the phone. She can't hold the receiver to her head and she won't let anyone else do it for her. Her thoughts are a bit jumbled these days. She tried to dictate a letter to me but it was impossible. We nearly fell out over it.

She is in room 118 in Springfield Hospital. Come by soon.

Yours,
Edith Murphy

[e-mail to Marie Pelli 11/10/05]

mom—by now you know that alice is in bad shape. andy and i have been at the hospital everyday since we heard, about a week ago. alice is connected to all these tubes and monitors. i don't understand any of it. her body can't nourish itself anymore or something, so she's wasting away. it's so horrible. she's in and out of lucidity too. sometimes she asks andy about his homework, like they're back at WFS. it's destroying him—he's drinking again. i don't know what to do. i never knew him drunk. he's so ashamed. he goes for walks and when he comes home he smells like whiskey and his eyes are all puffy. then he just goes to bed. i'm afraid he's going to lose his job. i'm just afraid about everything. he came home drunk last night and called his dad and ended up just screaming at him. i thought a neighbor was going to call the police. mom i don't know what to do. call me when you get a chance. something else is rocking my world, too.—maya

NOVEMBER 18th, 2005

DEAR ALICE—
HOW'S THE DYING GOING? I'm sitting underneath
an old friend Mr. Cohen. THE INSANITY OF
LIGHT IS SHINING TONIGHT BAYBEE!

So here's my poem—

Robot Baby

I was a little satellite
shooting up and out
a one and only
isolated
the hugeness of life
plus the chaos of space
received in my pure sensation:
eyes for seeking
mouth for longing   This //

I'm sayi'
on the m

Cops '
the edge—
I'm sneaking
here under
blendin in w
tells me he

until the BIG Sweep a few years back Joop stinks
and I'm moving on. Goodbye Joop. Goodbye stinkin babas!
How's that for PSYKODRAMA DR T.??

Okay Alie now I'm bouncing against the
white bullie they drop the ball in front of goodbye
eye adios fighty! Goodbye asshole toward
HEY, WHERE'S THE PORN? Goodbye
Pow!

Goodbye restaurands but especially the one I worked at
And goodbye to the beautiful faces who
me up when I was down and to all the waitresses
I worked at for and peace belted to all the asshole Managers
and native bees Fuck you and goodbye to all the
drunken regulars who tipped me nicely to keep them in those
cups see you soon! I've been here and tequily shorter
since I got here it's 5 and 3 sheets to the wind
an I am comin your way! Care of the my
Please honk you and finish the job I still miserable
Has been that I am

AND NOT EVEN THIRTY YET!
goodbye to the avenue screaming down them in cabs
goodbye to the cabbies but especially the dude who
explained across to me and why Alice's all go to hell's
Goodbye to the side streets and the quiet journeys thy
invite me on goodbye to all the people in this
little questrada what the fuck are you all DOING
in there. Goodbye.

[black Sharpie on yellow legal pad. This letter was written in and around Times Square, New York, in the early morning of November 18th, 2005. It was never sent]

Dear ALICE— HOWS THE DYING GOING? I'm sitting underneath an old friend Mr. Cohan. The INSANITY OF LIGHT IS SHINING TONIGHT BAYBEEEE! So here's my poem—

~~Rocket Baby~~
~~I was a little satellite~~
~~shooting up and out~~
~~a one and only~~
~~isolated~~
~~the hugeness of life~~
~~was the chaos of space~~
~~received in my pure sensations:~~
~~eyes for searching~~
~~mouth for longing~~
~~hands for reaching~~
~~heart for leaving~~ THIS <u>SUCKS</u> !!!

I'm saying goodbye. Goodbye big-titted babe on the marquee! Goodbye eye aching

Cops just made me move, but I've got the edge—FUCKING PIGS! I'm sneaking hiding I got a little place right here under the Lunt-Fontayne, yeah man I'm just blendin in with the hobos my man Joop here tells me he been hanging here for years until the Big Sweep a few years back Joop stinks and I'm moving on. Goodbye Joop! Goodbye stinking hobos!

How's this for PSYCHODRAMA DR T???

Okay Alice now I'm leaning against the big white building they drop the ball in front of. Goodbye eye aching lights! Goodbye asshole tourists!

HEY WHERE'S THE PORN? Goodbye porn!

Goodbye restaurants but especially the one I worked at Blue Angel goodbye to the beautiful fairies who lifted me up when I was down and to all the waitresses I lusted after and never bonked to all the asshole managers and maitre dees fuck you and goodbye to all the drunken regulars who tipped me nicely to keep them in their cups see you soon! It's been beer and tequila shooters since I got here at 5 and 3 sheets to the wind am I and comin your way! Come to take my place beside you and finish the job failed miserable has been that I am

AND NOT EVEN THIRTY YET!

goodbye to the avenues screaming down them in the cabs goodbye to the cabbies but especially the dude who explained auras to me and why the aliens all go to Marquee goodbye to the side streets and the quiet journeys they invite me on goodbye to all the people in their little apartments what the fuck are you all DOING in there Goodbye.

Cops again! They're FUCKING EVERYWHERE! CANT A MAN STAND IN TIMES SQUARE AND WRITE A DRUNK LETTER TO HIS DYING FRIEND? HAVE YOU NO HEART? OR MEANING?

Starbucks it is. 24 hour Starbucks. Gotta love that. Nose ring barrista is giving me the evil eye I will now curse her in print: SI VA ZOTAY ZENDEYQUA my trendy bitch! Leave me to my Jerkacheff and my misery. Goodbye trendy New York bitches. God I wanted to to to whatever goodbye.

Goodbye to all the other dreams the one about the Fool For Love revival with me as Eddy and the one about meeting Jennifer Aniston at the restaurant and hitting it off and her getting me cast in the Friends spin-off and me being a bigger deal than her and developing my own series leading to the movie that takes my career in a surprisingly serious direction directed by Eastwood and co-starring Uma who's hot for me even though I'm shorter than her and the oscar and the wedding and the happily ever BULLSHIT GOODBYE GOODBYE GOODBYE

Goodbye to the loeasaida artists who are stronger than I and can stick it out. I salute you with a sip of expensive coffee and I offer you this poem:

O my tender young artists
open up open up
follow your every instinct
~~be a free wheeling~~
be a living electric guitar

let the feelings linger
~~over hot coffee steam~~
like a girl falling out of love
embrace the rhythm of your life
like seasons changing
and you dancing
like a beating heart

CALL THIS ONE
"AFTER RILKE"

Hey New Jorkers—I want to be like you I wanted so badly to be
cool and tough like you to be joined with you to be on the same
side as you to be connected to you to be liked by you lifted up by
you fighting the good fight with you cheering you cheering me on
it just never happened and I only felt more and more alone

To all the tears on 83rd street goodbye your sacrifice was
in vain

To the hungry ghost—you win. I am eaten up. There's nothing
left but bones. Go suck on someone else.

Goodbye to all the spirits walking past this coffee house window
at 4 am WHAT ARE YOU DOING UP AT THIS HOUR? Each of you is such
a compelling mystery to me. Compelling mystery shit I must be
sobering up. Compelling mystery.

You are the sea above the sidewalk
I wade through you everyday
You sing a song I seem to know
I watch you trying so hard
~~You are the~~
I pass through your love and madness
I think: (Bing!)
This is who we are
Sometimes I feel choked
and I'm plagued by
the critical gibbon
ranting on my shoulder.
Sometimes I feel destined for
a life of little heartbreaks.
Then sometimes you

~~all of you~~
peel my eyes open,
you swell up around me
and I am a sad little island
no longer.

Sometimes—
if I awaken from the right kind of sleep—
there is clarity
like a deep and easy breath.
When I tap into it
strangers become delightful,
like wise and loving clowns.
The pink cheeks, the crows feet,
the giggle and the distant gaze
are stories for me to read,
or prayers to a greater mystery.

Bing!
It's a moment of
common rapture,
and I catch a glimpse
of God in your eyes,
in the corners of your mouths,
as you pass by.

CALL THIS "THE
GIGGLE AND THE
DISTANT GAZE"

7 am and Peter Pan taking me home. Sleepy Jersey a blur behind
turnpike barricades. This is the letter I never sent you Alice, written
in weakness and despair, just like the first one. Here's your poem.

Anything but walk away
it's a visitation of emptiness
and I become one of the stray dogs
fearful and unchained

if this loneliness was my home
maybe I'd be used to it by now

it's the sudden return that hurts
crashing down like old dusty mugs
useless and forgotten
they lie there in pieces

where are you?

sometimes I want to put a stick in your eye,
okay?
I get so angry that I love you so much
I become the sullen little boy I was
mute and diffident
with a solitude so huge
there are no tears to release it

ANYTHING BUT
WALK AWAY

come here and slap me around
chain me to the fence with my bowl
do anything
anything but walk away.

✺

but maybe it's not about you at all, Alice

[e-mail to Andy 11/20/05]

Andy—I arrive 3:58 United flight 173 from San Francisco. I'm staying at The Raddison. I'll call you when I get there.—Dad.

[the following is a transcription from a tape-recording made of Alice Jones on the evening of November 25th, 2005, by Edith Murphy while Alice was in the Springfield Hospital. Earlier that day, Andy, Maya Pelli, and Andy's father David Fallon spent an hour with Alice in her room. Also present during that visit were Edith, and Alice's sister Sarah Shelly. This cassette tape came to Andy with a note in blue ballpoint pen on white stationery, "Springfield Hospital, 'A Tradition of Caring'" printed on top:

Nov. 25, '05—Dear Andy, In lieu of letter, thought you'd like this. Edith]

Television is audible in the background.

Edith   I think it's on. [*Tape recorder is audibly set on a table.*]

Alice   Hello Andy.

Edith   Andy's not here.

Alice   Yes, I know that . . . I was speaking to the tape recorder . . . Well, I can't write anymore Andy. So I thought I'd ramble away for a few minutes, just to tell you how sweet it was . . . to see you [*long pause*] to see you this . . . morning . . . Your father is a good man.

Edith   Handsome too. What a looker.

Alice   Edith says your father is handsome.

Edith   Well, I think it's recording me too, Alice.

Alice   What?

Edith   Never mind. [*long pause*] Come on now, you don't want to send him a blank tape.

Alice   Sorry. I was distracted by the . . . by the abomination. Turn it off, will you Edith? [*TV is turned off*] That's better . . . I know why you stopped going to those meetings, Andy. You're not used to order. You're not used to pace, to . . . to. . . . Part of healing is not enjoying the chaos so much. Like Barbara said, don't be addicted to the intensity. You deserve a long, slow . . . you deserve order, but it doesn't matter what I say, you must decide you're worthy . . . to be healthy. . . . Anyway [*long pause*] life can be boring . . . very, very boring . . . but nothing's more boring than dying. Don't be fooled by the crap you see in the movies, it's tough and frightening especially when . . . especially when . . .

Edith Here's a tissue.

Alice [*inaudible*] . . . can't get a grip, it's slipping . . . I hate him. He's just at the beginning damn him . . . I'm at the end . . .

Edith There, there. You don't hate him. You love him. [*long pause*]

Alice I know. [*long pause*] The big messages unfold without you knowing . . . without you seeing them, and in between you go to work, you go to your . . . you go to meeting, or church or synagogue, whatever, you just go, and don't ask why. It's less about faith and more about practice, the faith comes from the practice, practice is something you do, everyday, because your *mind*, your *mind* . . . will confuse you. But your feet will take you there . . . Get me some water, will you love?

Edith Here. [*long pause*]

Alice You never had any pace in your life, Andy. It was all . . . zig-zaggy, life jumped out at you from behind corners. You think you don't deserve it. I mean the slow stuff, the order. Well, that's your work, my boy. No one's going to convince you of that but *you* . . . that you deserve it . . . a nice, slow life . . . regular . . . like poops. [*Alice and Edith can be heard laughing*]

Edith You know, I don't know how to erase things from that tape.

Alice You mean you're not Nixon's secretary? What was her name . . .

Edith No, I'm yours. I'm your lady in waiting for Pete's sake. [*long pause*]

Alice I miss Daddy . . . He died in the snow . . . We're going to a show together . . . I wish I could see you in the play Andy. God, I hate being trapped here, I just want to get this over with. . . . Make sure you touch them . . .

Edith Who?

Alice Well, the audience of course . . . there's no other reason. . . . Where'd he go?

Edith Who?

Alice Andy.

Edith He left this afternoon. . . . He came by with Maya and his father . . . Sarah was here.

Alice Oh God, the food was awful. I'm so sorry. Can you imagine? Sliced turkey from the deli with warm gravy on it. A travesty.

Edith I don't think they came here for the food.

Alice Sarah was here. Does Andy know about Sarah?

Edith Well, he knows she's your sister.

Alice Yes, but does he know the whole story?

Edith I don't know, why don't you tell him.

Alice Sarah and I have been estranged for a long time Andy. . . . She ran away from home . . . she escaped . . . my Mother . . . Sarah escaped and left her to me . . . met Jack—

Edith —her husband—

Alice Her husband, let me tell the story, will you? . . . Anyway, they ran off together, I had just been denied tenure. . . . Mother was ill . . . and the old dame just hung in there . . . for years . . . and I guess I just took care of her while Sarah and Jack set up shop . . . they lived in Bethesda . . . Jack had something to do with the Government . . .

Edith State Department.

Alice Well he doesn't need all the boring details. . . . Anyway, they have three precious children . . . Amy, Nick and . . . and . . .

Edith You want my help or not? [*long pause*] Julia. They're coming tomorrow. . . .

Alice I was so angry at her . . . she escaped and I was left behind . . . making sure Mother didn't hurt herself . . . I might have gone to New York with Dale . . . we were, you know. [*long pause*] Do you know, Edith, that Mother refused to lock the doors? This was the seventies in Germantown and the neighborhood was changing. But la, la, la Mother just left the doors wide open . . . I came by one afternoon and she was sitting in her kitchen talking to these alarming looking negroes . . . very well dressed but very severe and they wore their sunglasses inside the house . . . They were very polite. . . . Mother had made them lemonade . . . They had opened a Mosque up the street . . .

Edith Was she ever robbed?

Alice Never. Not once. So she kept her doors wide open.

Edith Bet those gentlemen looked out for her.

Alice My goodness, I never thought of that. Do you think so?

Edith Yes M'am. That's what I think. Why she was never robbed.

Alice I shall have to find them and thank them. [*long pause*] Let's see what's on the TV.

Edith You were telling Andy about Sarah.

Alice Is Andy here?

Edith No. The tape recording.

Alice Oh yes . . .oh yes . . . I was angry with Sarah, Andy . . . and she with me . . . and then after Mother died . . . 1978 . . . we would speak on the phone . . . the occasional Christmas . . . it was always tense . . . she left the Friends . . . she adopted a way of life that was very . . . it was . . . un-Quakerly . . .

Edith Here we go.

Alice Well, it was, it was, I'm sorry, but she had all these *things* and Jack drove around in these enormous cars and . . . and . . .

Edith And you were envious.

Alice Shut up, will you, that's enough . . . it was another Angel to wrestle, that's all . . . but she was here today and . . .

Edith That's good, that's good. My, my you're crying buckets today, here . . .

Alice It was so good to see her. She cried too.

Edith We all did. It was a big weepy mess in here. [*long pause*] Is there anything else you want to tell Andy on his tape recording?

Alice Yes . . . I want to tell him that he has authenticity . . . and this is what frightens people about him . . . it's his authenticity . . . he has no guile . . . no artifice . . . no mask . . . it comes directly out of him unfiltered, unimpeded . . . it is a burden and a responsibility he must bear . . . he is a natural Quaker, he speaks with integrity . . . God, he must be hard to live with . . . that Maya is something isn't she? You know she's pregnant.

Edith What?

Alice She doesn't know I know but I know . . . she looked at me funny today. . . authenticity. . . she's got her own flavor . . . when you accept it in yourself, you can speak without speaking . . . did you hear Andy's ministry in 1988? . . . I was there . . . He rose and spoke at Meeting for Worship, never spoken in Meeting before . . . he vibrated . . .

Edith Goodness.

Alice He was just shaking from the force of it . . .he stood and gripped the pew in front of him . . . and he said "There is darkness and there is light. And even though the darkness sucks me down, I choose the light." And then he sat down . . .

Edith What was he talking about?

Alice Who knows? He was twelve years old . . . His mother was . . . well, anyway . . . it was very powerful, sent a jolt through me, he did . . . that was the first time I felt it . . . the authenticity . . . I am a prophet . . .

Edith Really.

Alice I *am* a prophet! I am a prophet!

Edith Okay. Don't shout.

Alice Well I *will* shout! I come to proclaim a new Testimony! To add to Equality, to Simplicity, to Integrity, to Stewardship, to Peace! I come to proclaim the Testimony of Creativity! In all things let us be creative! Let us innovate! Let us give birth over and over! To designs and dances, to patterns and gardens and plays and performances and minuets and symphonies and songs and poems and proclamations! To movements and moments and . . . marches . . .

Edith Easy.

Alice Let us add the color of God to our houses. God is not grey! Or She is but He's also blue and green and black and bright . . . yellow! Get me a box of Crayons, I'll show you God! Let us teach all children to make to make to make . . . to make what they want to make! We must guide them! What they are led to make! We have to help them make themselves through the things they make! We have to help them make the world! The Testimony of Creativity! You will not hold me back! I will bring love and loss and longing to the world through my art! Do you hear me? You will not hold me back! It is God's work I do!

Edith Easy now.

Alice It's God's work . . . They all tried to hold me back . . . but I flew away . . . bright bird . . . I was a bright bird . . .

Edith Still are.

Alice Bright Quaker bird, that's me . . . get them to add Creativity to the list, will you Edith?

Edith I'll do my best.

Alice Well that's all I can ask for. [*long pause*]

Edith Anything else you want to add?

Alice To what?

Edith To the tape recording?

Alice Yes. I want to tell Andy why I demanded letters . . . I've saved them all, Andy . . . all your letters . . . so you have a record of your . . . this . . . what a long way you've come . . . when you see it . . . the shape of your life . . . get off the raft now . . . walk on solid ground and . . . make peace with who you are . . . becoming. [*long pause*] I'm tired.

Edith Okay. I'll turn it off. Say "bye."

Alice Bye . . . I love you . . . [*sound of tape-recorder being turned off*]

[e-mail to Marie Pelli 12/8/05]

hey mom—so good to see you last week. and so good that you caught alice
awake and with it. i have to tell you this amazing thing that happened. you
know alice was always getting andy to tell her about the play he's in with theater exile *Beyond Therapy*, about the performances, the little theater where they
play, etc. etc. so andy calls her at the hospital one night on his cell phone from
back stage. alice's sister sarah answers. andy tells her to hold the phone to
alice's ear, and to get comfortable. then he tells alice he's taking her to a show.
then andy puts the PHONE IN THE BREAST POCKET OF HIS BLAZER AND WALKS ON
STAGE! he did the whole show WITH THE PHONE ON and in his blazer pocket! and
alice heard the play, heard the audience laughing! sarah said she sat bolt
upright in her bed and giggled like a crazy person for almost an hour. then she
fell asleep. HOW COOL IS THAT? she sleeps a lot. i think it's close now.

he's got 18 days back in AA. being with his dad really helped. jeez it's been an
intense month.

and about, well, um, you know (woops!). andy and i went to meeting together
at 4th and arch and it just became so clear to me that it really wasn't an acci-
dent. andy's plate is a little full now, so he has a hard time talking about it. but
last night he threw his arms around me in bed and asked "how are you doing?
both of you?"

i said we're fine, just fine. and yourself?

and he said, better and better. then he put his hand on my belly.

i need to be with you more mom. see you tomorrow. love love love

maya

⟋⟍

[transcript of Andrew Fallon's vocal ministry from notes taken by Linda Emlin Berkowitz at the Meeting for Worship in memory of Alice Jones, December 22nd, 2005, Wallingford Friends' Meeting. Alice died December 15th 2005. These notes were edited for clarity with Andy's help]

Andy rises to speak. He cries.
Bear with me Friends . . . this may take a while . . .
Maya holds his hand.
I really don't feel like she's gone. I really don't. And that's not just wishful thinking. Some people just stick with you, and Alice is all over me like an old quilt. [*He cries.*] A quilt with the most beautiful colors. Some are faded and warm. Some are so bright. For the rest of my life, I will be able to wrap her around me, when I need her, when I miss her.

I've been sitting here trying to find the message of her life, some little gem I could share with you that would encapsulate what she stood for, what she meant to me and the people who loved her. But she was too complex, too human to fit in to any box. And maybe this is part of her message. Alice resembled the art she loved, the art she practiced, the art she taught—the art of acting. She was all over the place, messy and unpredictable. She resisted any dogma, any attempt to explain something neatly and completely, because then she would have nowhere to go, no room to explore. Alice taught me that acting and time are inextricably linked, and just as there is no such thing as the present, time being always in motion, so, too, acting may never be pinned down. It evades you, but if you love it the way Alice and I do, you just keep chasing it, joyfully, playfully.

She taught me that acting and life are inextricably bound. That acting cannot be studied in a vacuum, cannot be learned theoretically. It must be learned experientially and must be informed by the full fragrance of the earth and its creatures. The sensations of life, the events of the world, the creation of other artists, the edicts of politicians, the despair of your neighbors, the joy of your friends: these shape an actor's creativity, and the more alive and engaged in the world, the greater the actor. She showed me that the actor's most essential task is to move the other person, both real and fictional, and be moved in return.

She taught me that acting and self are inextricably bound. I am the actor, and the history of that "I" will be present through a veil in every character I play. Perhaps her greatest gift to me was showing me how that history could torment me and ruin my art if I let it, and how with some extra help, that history, no matter how grim in places, could be the fuel of creativity, could itself transform, and be the source of compassion and courage, not despair. She showed me that the care I take of myself has a direct impact on the quality of my teaching and my art. It's not so much what you teach, Alice said, but who you are.

A while back, Alice and I wrote to each other about "ripples"—those expanding circles of spiritual energy we send and receive, and here's another gift from Alice: how acting is deeply spiritual. I feel the ripples everywhere now. But they are especially amplified in some special places. This room and others like it, rehearsal rooms, classrooms and theaters, and anywhere I am with those I love.

Finally, Alice taught me that God is in my acting. So here is my prayer:

God, help me live a life worthy of the love I received from my dear friend Alice Jones. Help me be a vessel for Your light and power, and be a conduit for Your ripples. And help me remember to ask: who do You need me to be? I am an actor. I can be anyone. Who do You need me to be?

He sits.

For Andy:

"Be patterns, be examples
in all countries, places,
islands, nations, wherever
you come; that your
carriage and life may
preach among all sorts
of people, and to them.
Then you will come to
walk cheerfully over
the world, answering
that of God in everyone."
— George Fox

Or something like that!

Love,
Alice

[Note card with the image of the Moscow Art Theatre's program for their American tour in 1923 on the cover: gold and black color scheme with "THE MOSCOW ART THEATRE" above a white, art deco seagull. Sarah Shelly found this card while going through Alice's belongings. The card came with a letter, written in a graceful script resembling Alice's, blue ballpoint pen on embossed stationery, "The Quad, Swarthmore, Pennsylvania" printed on the top of the page]

January 5th, 2006

Dear Andy,
Found this in one of Alice's drawers. Thought you should have it.
In my eleventh hour re-connection with my sister, I came to understand how much you meant to her. Thanks for the comfort and purpose you gave her in her last year. Let's stay in touch.

Yours,
Sarah Shelley

Inside the note card, Alice's script in black fountain pen]

For Andy:
"Be patterns, be examples in all countries, places, islands, nations, wherever you come; that your carriage and life may preach among all sorts of people, and to them. Then you will come to walk cheerfully over the world, answering that of God in everyone."—George Fox
Or something like that!

Love,
Alice

∾

AFTERWORD

This book was born from the frustration of a previous book, a book I was writing for other people, according to rules and expectations I barely understood. It was a book about acting and the teaching of it called *Training the Total Actor*. It examined Stanislavsky, pedagogical techniques in the acting classroom, and what I called "The Unexplored Territories": the ways actors hurt themselves through acting, the intersection of the work of Bradshaw and Miller with this problem, the actor/director relationship, Psychodrama, and the concept of the "citizen actor." It was trying to be scholarship critical of the intellectual. It was a book at cross-purposes, and like so much of the writing about acting, it was dry and cold. After three drafts, I felt it was done, and essentially lifeless. And yet something kept calling to me about it, like a friend shouting to me from deep in the woods at the other side of the field. *People*—I realized, at the last minute—like the art I love, this book needs *people*. And so Andy and Alice walked out of the woods, and we got to work on *The Actor's Way*.

With *The Actor's Way*, I returned to Stanislavsky as my guide, who understood that a textbook for actors is counter-productive, and so he did something creative instead: he wrote a novel about an acting class. He knew that the unfolding drama of Tortsov's classroom would engage his creative audience much more than a step-by-step instruction in his "system"—a concept he was deeply suspicious of anyway. He also brought to life the relationship between the student and the teacher in his books, and his deep understanding of the student actor's journey and the teacher's charge is beautifully represented in that dual narrative. *The Actor's Way* is my humble attempt to represent that dynamic relationship in a twenty-first-century context. I find Stanislavsky's books impossible to teach from, mostly because I find the narrative more interesting than the exercises described. *The Actor's Way* similarly buries "techniques" and "approaches" beneath the life journeys of the two main characters. But I am perhaps trying to have it both ways. I have offered some handouts and exercises gleaned from my years of teaching acting in the hope that teachers reading this book will find them useful.

I am often affected more by the drama of the acting class itself and less by the scenes presented. That fascination is represented here. A central premise of mine is that in creative process, the teacher and what is taught cannot be separated. One deeply informs and transforms the other. In order to understand the teaching, you must be in the room with the teacher. I have tried to bring to life the rooms Andy and Alice lived and worked in, and represent "the dynamic collision of souls" Alice speaks of when she describes what ideally happens between a teacher and a student. I also believe that acting, and the study and teaching of it, can transform people, and those transformations change the world, one relationship at a time. So the small constellation of relationships around Alice and Andy are as germane to this study of acting as is anything that happens in the classroom. I wish to paint the picture of artists' art changing artists' lives, and the lives of those they touch.

My other "template" is Rilke's *Letters to a Young Poet*, a beautiful collection of letters on creativity and the struggle of the artist, a book I return to again and again. I have been so affected by Rilke's efforts to help to the young Mr. Kappus, and have gradually wished I could have read Mr. Kappus' letters, as well. In *The Actor's Way*, I have included both the novice and the mentor's letters, and have been guided by Rilke's intensely personal and spiritual tone.

At my core, I am an actor, and looking back, I see now that what I have done in *The Actor's Way* is act through writing. My creativity is best expressed through the guise of characters. So I have created characters in this book and spoken through them in the first person, giving them my ideas to play with, to argue about, to explore. *The Actor's Way* is a strange blend of fiction, non-fiction, and memoir. I am none of the characters in this book, though I am in all of them. As personal as some of this book is, it is primarily based on observation: on years of living, working, and playing with actors and directors, and discerning what happens in classrooms and rehearsal halls. I hope Andy's flight from New York is not received as a condemnation of that city (the city of my birth and childhood), and I hope that my celebration of Philadelphia may be shared by the many other cultural communities across the country, urban or not, that make it possible to be a Citizen Artist.

I wish the book's examination of Quakerism to be the beginning of a broader discussion about the relationship between spirituality and creativity. This spirituality can take many forms, and I don't mean to imply that one must become a Quaker to be a great actor or acting teacher. Quakerism, as I practice it and as described in Philadelphia Yearly Meeting's *Faith and Practice*, offers a uniquely universalist approach to spiritual seeking that I believe lends itself to applications in other areas. I hope artists and teachers who read this book may be inspired to ask questions about their own spiritual lives, and look for the means of spiritual exploration most suitable for them. I hope the Quakers who read it will gain an insight into the connection between creativity, performance, and ministry.

One of the greatest differences between my experience and Andy's is that I never had an Alice. But I feel I must credit some great older women I have known who danced around in my head while I wrote this: the great gardener, equestrienne, and print-maker Elizabeth Foster of Ipswich, Massachusetts, and Jackson, New Hampshire; Alice Mamarchev, my grade-school drama teacher; and Alice Brown, an elderly Quaker who had a deep and unexpected effect on me.

I wish to thank Nicole Potter-Talling and everyone at Allworth Press for believing in this book.

I wish to thank Haverford Friends Meeting in Haverford, Pennsylvania, for their spiritual sustenance and inspiration.

I wish to thank the Philadelphia Theatre Community, but especially People's Light & Theatre in Malvern, Pennsylvania, my primary artistic home. It is the place I first witnessed the Citizen Actor paradigm at work—though I didn't know what to call it then.

I wish to thank my Mom, the Naropa Institute dancer and teacher Barbara Dilley, who has shown me what it means to be a spiritual artist in the world; and my Dad, Lewis Lloyd, who raised me and instilled in me the virtues I pass on to my students, and who lovingly nudged me to keep writing.

I wish to thank Villanova University Professor Michael Hollinger, an accomplished playwright and dear friend, who was my cheerleader as I waded through the preparations for this book, and gave me wonderful notes. Villanova Professor Boris Briker helped me in matters regarding the translation of Stanislavsky's work.

My research assistant for that previous book was Villanova graduate student J. Cooper Robb, who never blinked, no matter how strange my requests were. He dug up many fine books to read and I am indebted to him. Early draft readers include Professor Cary Mazer, Ceal Phelan, Professor Lee Devin, David Grillo, Steven Wangh, and my Mom and Dad. Their thoughts were helpful and I thank them.

In the spring of 2002, I took a sabbatical in which I observed some fine acting teachers at work. Those observations and my conversations with those teachers have affected this book. My heartfelt thanks to: Bill Esper, Ron Van Lieu, Mark Hammer, Austin Pendleton, Anya Saffir, Talish Barrow, and Edith Meeks. My thanks also to their students who welcomed me, and whose work was brave and instructive.

This book was also affected by the 2002 Teacher Development Program at The Actors Center of New York. My thanks to the acting teachers who were my co-participants, many of whom also spoke with me about teaching: Meg Bussert, Mary Ann Colias, Mary Coy, Janice Dean, R. Scott Lank, Leah Lowe, Peder Mulhouse, Jim Ryan, Terry Stoecker, and Lars Tatum; and to our teachers in the workshop: Slava Dolgachev, Robert Cohen, Per Brahe, Peter Francis James, Dudley Knight, and Catherine Fitzmaurice.

I wish to especially acknowledge my own students, past and present. You inspire me.

Lastly, thanks to my wife, the extraordinary actress, teacher, and human being Susan Linder McKey, who is in these pages by virtue of her love and support of me, and for whom words seem insufficient.

—*Benjamin Lloyd*
Wynnewood, Pennsylvania   *November, 2005*

APPENDIX

Zing, Boing, Pow, Schlock
Learned from Mark McKenna, Touchstone Theatre, Pennsylvania

1. In a circle, a student turns to the student next to him quickly, clapping hands in the direction s/he's turning and says "Zing!" loudly. The student who has received the Zing turns to the next student and does the same thing. The Zing goes around the circle like this.
2. Only a Boing can make a Zing change direction. To execute a Boing, a student behaves like a rubber wall, facing the incoming Zing and yelling "Boing!" while holding his/her arms in a suitably wall-like manner. Then the person who has Zinged the Boinger either Zings in the reverse direction or Pows someone (see below).
3. Pow goes across the circle, or to anyone except the person directly to the left or right. It is the "cops and robbers" Pow, though I dissuade students from imitating guns, and ask for pointed index fingers instead. The person receiving the Pow may Zing to the left or right, Boing the Pow-er or Pow someone else. Or they may Schlock (see below).
4. Schlock is the bail-out. A student who has received any of the above may throw the energy on the floor in the middle of the circle yelling "Schlock!" The game continues when another student reaches for the energy laying in the middle of the circle, yelling "Got it!" and then executing either a Zing or a Pow.

   This is my favorite warm-up. It quickly becomes goofy and induces laughter. It teaches focus, intent and the necessity of having fun and going for it even when you make mistakes. I draw attention to the "mistakes" as a way to get the students to notice what happens to them when they are under pressure, and to suggest that there is as much to be learned from it going off the rails as there is from it moving along nicely.

Some of my variations include:
- As fast as possible
- World Wrestling Federation, or Super Hero version: completely exaggerated and over the top vocal and physical choices
- Bored Student version
- Polite version
- Telling students to go "Moooo!" all together along with a suitable cow-like gesture whenever someone makes a mistake

Repetition
Learned from Talish Barrow and Anya Saffir,
Atlantic Theatre Company School, NY.

1. Two students in front of the class sit facing each other. They are asked not to slouch, but to sit with a sense of presence.
2. Student A notices something about student B and says it. Student B repeats it. Student A repeats the observation, etc. Example:
   - You're wearing a red shirt.
   - I'm wearing a red shirt.
   - You're wearing a red shirt.
   - I'm wearing a red shirt.
3. This continues until student B notices something about student A and says it. So if the pair from above continued, it might go something like this:
   - You're wearing a red shirt.
   - I'm wearing a red shirt.
   - You're wearing a red shirt.
   - You have earrings.
   - I have earrings.
   - You have earrings.
   - Etc.
4. It is important that the students do not deviate from the established words used. For example, with our pair above, student B shouldn't say "Yeah, I got a red shirt on." Part of what is being investigated is the limited language available, and what rises up unselfconsciously through the repetition. It's also important that they adhere to a rhythm. The rhythmic quality stimulates reactions from the participants they have no control over, which is the point.

Students should be urged to stay with it even if they crack up or feel embarrassed, a useful learning point for student actors who are prone to drop out of situations that make them uncomfortable. This is the basic exercise originally developed by Sanford Meisner. I have developed some variations:

- After the basic form has been learned, I encourage my students to make "personal observations:" "You look sad—I look sad" or "You have a nice smile—I have a nice smile." I stress that under no circumstances will observations used to humiliate or embarrass be tolerated.
- I ask students to stand and do the exercise. I ask them to move around the room and do the exercise.
- For classes with a high degree of trust: I ask them to tell lies about each other. "You have a pet monkey—I have a pet monkey" or "You're the Queen of Sheba—I'm the Queen of Sheba."
- These variations are meant to raise the level of vulnerability experienced, as well as increase the multi-tasking challenges faced. In all these variations, students are asked to stay in the exercise no matter what, to get out of the way of whatever arises naturally from within, and to avoid the temptation to manufacture attitudes or characterizations. Genuine revealing of human behavior is the goal.

The Red Square
Learned from Barbara Dilley, The Naropa Institute, CO.

1. Tape down a large red square on the floor. Red yarn is best: it's bright and makes a thicker line to demarcate the square. A square made entirely of tape is messy to clean up.
2. Present the Red Square as sacred space. Use your own language for this. Relate it to theater. Relate it to spirituality.
3. Ask the students to see themselves in a frozen pose in relation to the Red Square (this can mean in it, outside of it, or on the line itself).
4. When a student has a vision which seems clear, they follow an impulse to rise, go to that position and embody it. They hold that pose for a moment or two, then sit down. Continue until each student has gone.
5. Variations:
   - Duets: in which student A holds the pose until a second student poses in relation to it. Then the duet pose melts and the sequence begins again with two other students.

- The river: in which a student begins with a pose, and other students respond free-form, so that many students may be in and around the square at the same time, dropping in and out when they feel moved to.
- The rush: in which one student strikes a pose, then after several seconds, the teacher claps hands and the entire class poses simultaneously around that original pose.
- Add furniture, props and small costume pieces to the Square, and invite poses that incorporate these elements.
- Add text, and invite poses in which text is spoken.

6. Questions:
   - How comfortable are students with poses that are abstract, not obvious? What is the theatrical difference between an obvious and an abstract pose?
   - What was the impulse you felt that made you get up and pose? How does that impulse relate to acting generally? How does the pose relate to acting generally?
   - How do solos and duets and rivers differ from each other? What happens when props, text, etc., are added? Is creativity enhanced or diminished?

The Grid
Learned from Barbara Dilley, The Naropa Institute, CO.

1. Students are instructed to move as if there is a giant imaginary grid on the floor. In a conventional rectangular classroom, half the lines are parallel to one set of walls, half parallel to the other set. The dimensions of the grid itself are unimportant (it's imaginary). So teachers should be unconcerned with size of the squares the grid makes, for example. You are setting up a movement pattern in the room in which students are moving in straight lines and turning at right angles. The grid doesn't support students moving in circles on the floor, or moving diagonally.
2. Once students are comfortable simply walking around on the grid (it will have a slightly military quality at first), you can then add movement suggestions. Backwards, forwards, sideways, fast, slow, high, low. You can ask for movement qualities: rounded, jumpy, angular, heavy. Make them use their arms!
3. You can encourage encounters in the grid: imitating, following, leading. You can encourage playing without imitating (i.e., contrast or opposition)—an

important challenge. You can add sounds or words and see what happens when language is introduced to encounters in the grid. I use "Yes, no, maybe, me, you," which students can use in any combination.

The grid is a useful way to get students to loosen up physically and explore their bodies in space. It provides a framework, which gives them a sense of safety, and introduces a discipline (you have to stay on the grid). You can relate the grid to a script: it is a framework, it has boundaries and limitations, and yet within it, there are enormous possibilities.

It also introduces a way for students to play together, in the childlike sense of that word. Encourage students to get goofy and silly (go ahead, do the Macarena!) Point out how much more creative they become when they are having fun. Tip: don't let them imitate each other for too long. It breeds laziness and mockery. Demand that they make choices.

Grouping
Learned from Slava Dolgachev, New Theater, Moscow

In this exercise, a student is simply asked to take each member of the class by the hands and place them with other members in groups that make sense to him/her. The student is asked to work quickly and not to ponder how to make "perfect" groups. Each student takes a turn grouping the class. As Alice points out, it's the physical contact that matters. The students will be too focused on what the groups "mean" to be self-conscious about being touched. This is a good way to build safety and ensemble early on.

Remembering Hands
Learned from Slava Dolgachev, New Theater, Moscow

1. Everyone removes rings, and watches and rolls up their sleeves. The class is instructed to examine each others' hands. They are told they will be asked to identify hands, blindfolded. They are to stand and mill around each other, taking each hand they encounter and studying it, paying special attention to the way it feels. Chit-chat and joking is to be kept at a minimum. All focus should be on the hands.

2. After some initial exploration, they should begin to work with their eyes closed. They should pull students close together who have similar hands so that they can find ways of telling them apart.

3. After about five minutes of this, more or less depending on the size of the class, a volunteer is asked for. The volunteer stands blindfolded in front of the class, who then mix themselves up, to ensure the volunteer hasn't memorized placement in the room.

4. The teacher silently points to a student, who approaches the blindfolded student. The teacher places the students' hands in each others'. The blindfolded student is asked to guess out loud whose hands he/she is holding. If he guesses right, the student in question says "Yes!" If he guesses wrong, the student in question says nothing and returns to the group.

5. This goes on until the teacher feels it has run its course. In a large class, not everyone may get a chance to wear the blindfold.

This exercise also builds ensemble through safe touching, and it begins to explore Stanislavsky's Rays. Students can be asked to let the blindfolded one know who they are without a vocal or physical signal of any kind, a kind of "spirit identification." Teachers are encouraged to invite questions, rather than provide answers to explorations of this kind. It's the searching that matters most.

The exercise also has a useful application in exploring creative impulse. Frequently, the students who guess right most reliably do so quickly. They trust their first impulse. Students who struggle tend to linger with hands, and frown and bite their lips. A line can be drawn between the successful blindfolded apprehending of identity and the expression of a spontaneous creative impulse.

BIBLIOGRAPHY AND WORKS CITED

Arrien, Angeles. *The Four-Fold Way* (San Fransisco: Harper Collins, 1993)

Bates, Brian. *The Way of the Actor* (Boston: Shambhala Publications, 1987)

Birkel, Michael. *Silence and Witness* (Maryknoll, NY: Orbis Books, 2004)

Bradshaw, John. *Healing the Shame That Binds You* (Deerfield, FL: Health Communications, Inc., 1988)

Brinton, Howard. *Friends for 350 Years* (Wallingford, PA: Pendle Hill, 2002), With Margaret Hope Bacon.

Bruder et al. *A Practical Handbook for the Actor* (New York: Vintage, 1986)

Carnicke, Sharon Marie. *Stanislavsky in Focus* (The Netherlands: Harwood Academic Publishers, 1998)

Chekhov, Anton. *Uncle Vanya* and *The Seagull* in *The Plays of Anton Chekhov*, trans. by Paul Schmidt (New York: Harper Perennial, 1999)

Durang, Christopher. *Beyond Therapy* (New York: Nelson Doubleday, 1981)

Faith & Practice, Philadelphia Yearly Meeting, The Religious Society of Friends, revised 1997.

Finding Nemo, Disney/Pixar (2003), Andrew Stanton, director.

Garden State, Fox Searchlight/Miramax (2004), Zack Braff, director.

Heavenly Creatures, Miramax (1994), Peter Jackson, director.

Hughes, R.G. "Tolstoy, Stanislavski, and the Art of Acting," *The Journal of Aesthetics and Art Criticism*, Volume 51, Issue 1 (Winter, 1993)

Jennings, Sue. *Introduction to Dramatherapy: Theatre and Healing, Ariadne's Ball of Thread* (Philadelphia: Jessica Kingsley Publishers, 1998)

The Journal of George Fox. Thomas Ellwood, ed. (Philadelphia: Philadelphia Yearly Meeting, 1997)

Kaufman, Moises. *The Laramie Project* (New York: Vintage Books, 2001)

Magarshack, David. *Stanislavsky: A Life* (London: Faber & Faber, 1986)

Mamet, David. *True and False* (New York: Vintage Books, 1997)

Mast, Sharon. *Stages of Identity: A Study of Actors* (London: Gower, 1986)

The Matrix, Warner Studios (1999), Andy Wachowski, Larry Wachowski, directors

Miller, Alice. *The Drama of the Gifted Child* (New York: Basic Books, 1981)

Moreno, J.L. *New Introduction to Psychodrama* (Boston: Beacon House, 1963)

Moreno, J.L. *The Discovery of the Spontaneous Man* (Boston: Beacon House, 1958)

Nigro, Don. *Glamorgan and Other Plays* (New York: Samuel French, Inc., 1996)

O'Neill, Eugene. *Long Day's Journey into Night* (New Haven, CT: Yale University Press, 1955)

O'Reilley, Mary Rose. *Radical Presence* (Portsmouth, NH: Boynton/Cook, 1998)

Palmer, Parker J. *The Courage to Teach* (San Francisco: Jossey-Bass, 1997)

Rilke, Ranier Maria. *Letters to a Young Poet*, trans. by M.D. Herter Norton (New York: W.W. Norton, 1996)

Roach, Joseph. *The Player's Passion* (Newark: University of Delaware Press; London: Associated University Presses, 1985)

Salinger, J.D. *Franny and Zooey* (New York: Little, Brown; 1991)

Scrubs, Touchstone Television, N.B.C.

Shanley, John Patrick. *Danny and the Deep Blue Sea* (New York: Dramatists Play Service, 1984)

Shepard, Sam. *Fool for Love and Other Plays* (New York: Bantam Books, 1984)

Stanislavsky, Constantine. *An Actor Prepares*, trans. by Elizabeth Reynolds Hapgood (New York: Theatre Arts Books, 1948)

Stanislavsky, Constantine. *Building a Character*, trans. by Elizabeth Reynolds Hapgood. (New York: Theatre Arts Books, 1949)

Stanislavski, Constantin. *My Life in Art*, trans. by J.J. Robbins (New York: Theatre Arts Books, 1948)

Stanislavsky's Legacy, edited and trans. by Elizabeth Reynolds Hapgood (New York: Routledge, 1999)

Tolstoy, Leo. *A Confession and Other Religious Writings*, trans. by Jane Kentish (New York: Penguin Putnam, 1987)

Williams, Tennessee. *The Glass Menagerie* in *Tennessee Williams Eight Plays* (New York: Nelson Doubleday, 1979)

ABOUT THE AUTHOR

Benjamin Lloyd is a theatre artist, writer, and teacher based in Philadelphia. Ben has an M.F.A. in Acting from the Yale School of Drama and has taught acting at Princeton and Villanova Universities, as well as numerous training programs attached to professional theatres. In addition to performing at every major theatre in Philadelphia, Ben has acted and directed in New York City, where he played Hamlet in *Qi Hamlet*; Edinburgh, Scotland, where he performed his own play *Psychodrama*; and Prague, the Czech Republic. He is a member of the Artistic Company at People's Light & Theatre in Malvern, PA and he lives in Wynnewood, Pennsylvania, with his wife and two children.

INDEX

A

Books from Allworth Press

Allworth Press is an imprint of Allworth Communications, Inc. Selected titles are listed below.

Letters from Backstage: The Adventures of a Touring Stage Actor
by Michael Kostroff (paperback, 6 x 9, 224 pages, $16.95)

Making It on Broadway: Actors' Tales of Climbing to the Top
by David Wienir and Jodie Langel (paperback, 6 x 9, 288 pages, $19.95)

Acting—Advanced Techniques for the Actor, Director, and Teacher
by Terry Schreiber (paperback, 6 x 9, 256 pages, $19.95)

Improv for Actors
by Dan Diggles (paperback, 6 x 9, 246 pages, $19.95)

Movement for Actors
edited by Nicole Potter (paperback, 6 x 9, 288 pages, $19.95)

Acting for Film
by Cathy Haase (paperback, 6 x 9, 240 pages, $19.95)

Acting That Matters
by Barry Pineo (paperback, 5½ x 8½, 240 pages, $16.95)

Mastering Shakespeare: An Acting Class in Seven Scenes
by Scott Kaiser (paperback, 6 x 9, 256 pages, $19.95)

The Art of Auditioning
by Rob Decina (paperback, 6 x 9, 224 pages, $19.95)

An Actor's Guide—Making It in New York City
by Glenn Alterman (paperback, 6 x 9, 288 pages, $19.95)

Promoting Your Acting Career, Second Edition
by Glenn Alterman (paperback, 6 x 9, 256 pages, $19.95)